CASTLES OF CU...

M.J. Jackson

Medieval Castles of England, Vol. 2

CAREL PRESS + **CUMBRIA COUNTY LIBRARY**

18 Chertsey Bank, Carlisle, CA1 2QF

1 872365 05 1

Designed and produced by Linda K. Graphic Design Studio, North Shields.

Cover: Piel Castle.
Inside front cover: Lammerside Castle stands on the fell side near the River Eden.

Egremont Castle: the 12th-century gatehouse. Note the herringbone masonry in the adjoining curtain wall.

PREFACE

This gazetteer is a record of all the county's known medieval castles, existing or destroyed, together with their location, a brief description and a condensed history. The bibliography for each site will enable those who wish, to delve deeper into the history and buildings of the more complex sites. For the purpose of this book a castle is any fortification founded between 1066 and 1600 which has always been called, or generally termed, a castle, and any building for which a Licence to Crenellate was issued. Towers, fortified houses, etc. not called 'castle', and which did not receive a Licence to Crenellate are not included in the main list though some may appear in the Appendix.

Descriptions are general in term and make no claim to be exact, though to the best of my knowledge they are correct. I have visited all of the sites in the gazetteer and also a number of those in the Appendix. No attempt has been made to describe interiors, contents or detail, this I leave to the more specialist castle or architectural publications. Plans are only included to assist the description and are not to scale, and do not necessarily show existing remains. Unless otherwise shown, the top of the plan is North. The Appendix is a list of 'castle' place names, etc. which I have come across during my research, and include buildings, hill-forts, etc., fieldnames, and earthworks previously considered to be castle sites but which recent documentary evidence and/or excavation have proved otherwise.

M.J. Jackson
Faugh
Carlisle
Cumbria

January 1990

Dedicated to my son Christopher

Brougham Castle: the keep.

CONTENTS

Page

Introduction   7 — 19

Index of Sites   21 — 25

Location Map   26

GAZETTEER   27 — 93

Appendix   95 — 101

Chronology   103 — 109

Scottish Monarchs   111

Bibliography   113 — 114

Glossary   115 — 119

Pennington Castle, an immensely strong ringwork.

The damaged motte, Aldingham.

INTRODUCTION

Since the departure of the Romans the art of fortification had been neglected by the English, who lived in some ex-Roman walled towns like Winchester or in settlements defended by a bank or ditch. Castles were introduced into England soon after 1042 by Norman friends of Edward the Confessor who accompanied him on his return from exile in Normandy; three were built in Herefordshire and one in Essex. The English nobles, however, mostly ignored this new concept of warfare which has since been described as 'the most formidable advance in military engineering that had been seen for generations'. It was not until after the battle of Hastings in 1066 that castles became a familiar sight all over England.

The four early castles of Herefordshire and Essex, built only of earth and timber, are thought to have been strong enclosures, now called 'ringworks', which were not necessarily circular as the name implies (Fig. 1). They were easily constructed by digging a ditch and throwing the material inwards to form a strong defensive bank, or breastwork, and consequently were quick, cheap and easy to build with the unskilled labour available. A palisade was erected along the top of the bank, and various wooden buildings were erected inside, such as a hall, which was the main

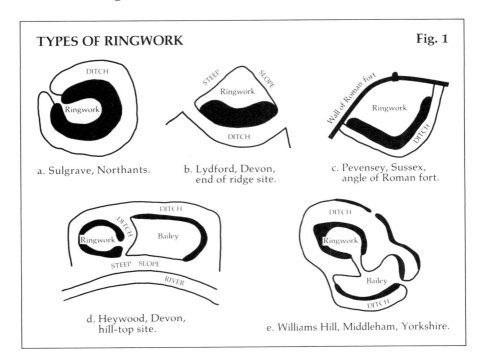

TYPES OF RINGWORK Fig. 1

a. Sulgrave, Northants.

b. Lydford, Devon, end of ridge site.

c. Pevensey, Sussex, angle of Roman fort.

d. Heywood, Devon, hill-top site.

e. Williams Hill, Middleham, Yorkshire.

A TYPICAL 11th or 12th CENTURY MOTTE AND BAILEY

Fig. 2

Plan and Elevation

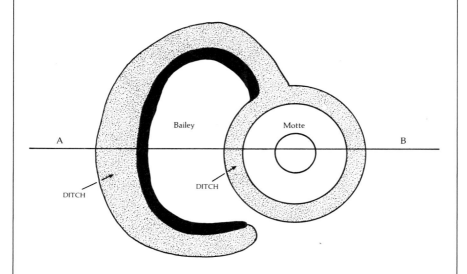

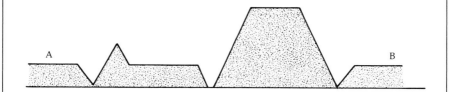

residence, a chapel, a stable and a workshop, and there was usually a very strong gateway approached over a drawbridge. Some of these ringworks had one or more enclosures, called baileys, attached to the side (Fig. 1d, 1e) which not only gave more space inside the ringwork, by the probable removal of the workshop and stable, but also gave space for the protection of cattle, etc. in times of trouble. The castle site was nearly always carefully chosen for its defensive strength, usually on highish ground and wherever possible close to, or on the bank of a river or stream, which not only provided water and served as an extra line of defence, but if large enough was a convenient supply route and, if necessary, a means of retreat. Ringworks in Cumbria can be seen at Castle Crag (Bampton), Coupland, Hayton (Brampton), Maryport, Pennington, and also at Cockermouth and Kendal, which were both rebuilt with masonry, and at Appleby and Brough castles which may have originated as a ringwork and bailey. With the exception of Kendal Castle, which is a hill-top site, all are situated at the end of a spur or promontory.

Another type of castle introduced by the Normans soon after the Conquest was the motte and bailey (Fig. 2), which consisted of a circular mound of earth (the motte) with one or more attached baileys. The motte was usually made by digging a ditch and throwing the material inwards to form a mound, but in some cases the banks were built up first as if making a ringwork and then in-filled to the required height, the bank ensuring greater stability (Fig. 3). Wherever possible the motte was adapted from a natural feature such as a hillock (or in some cases an old burial mound which would be well consolidated) by surrounding it with a ditch, levelling the top and steepening the sides. Sometimes the motte was built up around an existing tower to protect its base and at other times it was built up together with the tower. In some cases, such as at Aldingham situated in the south of the county, the existing ringwork was converted into a motte by in-filling and heightening (Fig. 3); in others, like Liddel Strength in north Cumbria which probably originated as a ringwork, the motte was built up over one side of the existing bank. The summit of the motte was enclosed with a palisade to protect a high wooden tower called a 'keep', and was usually reached from the bailey by a flying-bridge (i.e. a rising wooden bridge supported on stilts), the top section of which was a drawbridge. These keeps were not generally built for residential purposes but more as a place to keep valuables and weapons, and for use as a place of refuge when the rest of the castle had fallen to an enemy. Like the ringwork the motte and bailey was easy and cheap to build, and with unlimited labour could be built very quickly. A recorded instance of quick construction is that of the 11th century motte called 'Baille Hill' at York which is 12m high and was reputedly built in eight days! This has been suggested as an exaggeration on the part of early chroniclers, but it must be remembered that this was a royal castle being built at a critical time and with no shortage of manpower, and though it has been calculated that it would take fifty men working a ten-hour day in good weather, forty-two days to build a motte 5m high, these calculations of course do not include a life or death threat such as that to which the labourers of the motte at York would be under, no doubt increasing their efficiency.

The ringwork and the motte and bailey are the basis of nearly all our surviving castles and probably the best known example of the motte and bailey is Windsor Castle, built in 1069 and continuously occupied since. It is surprising that with the exception of those few isolated cases previously mentioned, the English made no attempt to copy the Normans by building their own castles. Their failure to do so was a major contribution to their defeat, as after the battle of Hastings they had nowhere strong enough to which to retreat and regroup, and if they had they could have forced William into a series of time wasting and money-consuming sieges which may have forced him to abandon the conquest.

Duke William of Normandy arrived at Pevensey on the shores of Sussex in September 1066 and immediately adapted the Roman fort there as a castle; he did this by making a ringwork in one corner of the fort (Fig. 1c), and utilising the remainder as a bailey. Soon after he erected another

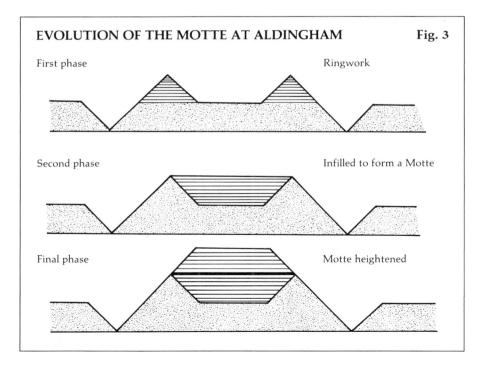

EVOLUTION OF THE MOTTE AT ALDINGHAM **Fig. 3**

First phase Ringwork

Second phase Infilled to form a Motte

Final phase Motte heightened

castle at Hastings, 11km to the east, and though this is shown on the Bayeaux Tapestry as a motte, it is considered more likely to have been a ringwork. He placed this castle in the care of Humphrey de Tilliol, possibly an ancestor of the founder of Scaleby Castle. After the battle of Hastings William advanced slowly on London, building castles as he progressed, and after his coronation at Westminster on the 25th December, he commenced extending his authority in all directions. By 1071 nearly forty major castles had been erected (there were probably many more minor ones), as far as York in the north-east, Chester in the north-west and Exeter in the south-west. Expansion proceeded apace and by 1086 William was closing in on Cumbria with castles to the east at Newcastle-upon-Tyne, Durham and Richmond, and to the south at Penwortham, near Preston and Clitheroe. In 1092 William II came north to take and annexe Cumberland from the Scots, and to settle it with men from the south; he also erected or caused to be erected, castles at Carlisle, Liddel Strength, Bewcastle and Brough, and probably at this time castles were built at Aspatria, Beaumont, Burgh by Sands, and Maryport. Two of these castles, Bewcastle and Brough utilised existing Roman fortifications just as William I had done at Pevensey, and Beaumont is built over a Roman milecastle.

Where stone was plentiful, such as at Brough where there was a ready cut supply from the Roman fort, castles were built with masonry straight away, but elsewhere castles generally continued to be built with timber, and only as conditions allowed were they rebuilt with masonry, becoming centres for local government, and usually containing the gaol. From c.1100 the small rectangular-shaped stone-built keep began to replace the earlier ones built of timber, and similarly were not necessarily for residential use. The foundations of one of these keeps were found at Brough Castle beneath the floor of the present large keep which was built c.1170. Because of its weight, the keep could not be built upon an artificially made motte and consequently in many places it replaced the motte as the ultimate strength of the castle. At some castles, usually of the ringwork type, the gatehouse was the strong point, and was the first structure to be rebuilt with masonry. In some cases such as at Ludlow Castle in Shropshire, the gatehouse was later converted into a keep by blocking up the entrance and making a new entrance beside it. During the troubled reign of King Stephen (1135-54) generally termed 'the Anarchy', hundreds of ringwork and motte and bailey castles were built by noblemen and landowners who not only fought for one of the opposing sides, but also frequently fought each other, and excavations have shown that many of these castles had a small stone-built keep. Many of these castles were 'adulterine' (built without the king's permission) and consequently many were destroyed or abandoned when Henry II came to the throne in 1154. During Henry's reign (1154-89) the great rectangular-shaped keep came into prominence,

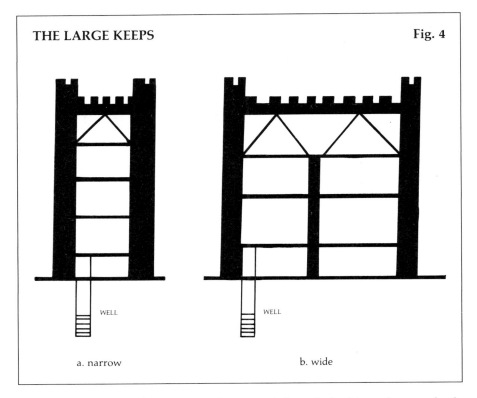

THE LARGE KEEPS   Fig. 4

WELL

WELL

a. narrow

b. wide

replacing the hall as the main residence, and though the king of course built many at his castles, others were built by the wealthier nobles at their castles. Good examples of this type of keep can be seen in Cumbria at Appleby, Brough and Brougham castles, all built c.1170. The walls of this type of keep varied in thickness between 2.44m and 4.57m and were generally 13.72m to 21.34m high, with an entrance at first floor level reached by a fixed stair usually defended and contained within a fore-building. The entrance usually opened directly into the principal room and from here a spiral stair in one or two of the angles (see Fig. 5e) gave access to the upper floors and to the roof, which generally had a steep pitch hidden from below by a high parapet (Fig. 4). In the thickness of the walls passages led to garderobes, or in those keeps with exceptionally thick walls, to small rooms (Fig. 5e), and in the wider of these large keeps (Figs. 4b and 5e) the interior was divided by a cross-wall to reduce the span for the wooden floor.

The rough average for building one of these large keeps has been estimated at about one year for the foundations and thereafter about 3m per year, depending on the complexity and also allowing for slower

KEEPS 1166-1262

Fig. 5

Not to uniform scale

a. Orford, Suffolk.
1166-72

b. Appleby, Cumbria.
1170

c. Chilham, Kent.
1171-4

d. Tickhill, Yorkshire.
1178-80

e. Dover, Kent.
1180-90

f. Conisbrough, Yorkshire.
1185

g. Longtown, Herefordshire.
c. 1187

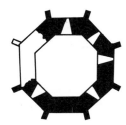

h. Odiham, Hampshire.
1207-11

i. Cliffords Tower, York.
1245-62

SHELL-KEEPS   **Fig. 6**

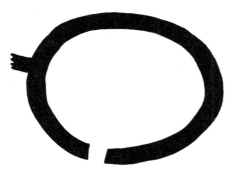

a. Trematon, Cornwall.
12c.

STEPS UP
SIDE OF
MOTTE

b. Launceston, Cornwall.
Outer wall 12c.
Inner wall c. 1227

c. Restormal, Cornwall.
12c. and 13c.

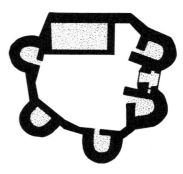

d. Clifford, Herefordshire.
c. 1180-1220

e. Snodhill, Herefordshire.
c. 1200

Not to uniform scale

progress as the walls became higher. Because the rectangular keep was vulnerable during a siege to miners (who undermined an angle causing it to collapse), angle buttresses were made solid up to first-floor level, or were built far enough forward so that flanking fire could be directed from their tops along each face of the keep so keeping the miners etc. at bay. Though these keeps were still being built as late as 1180, as early as 1166 the king was building a new type of keep at Orford Castle in Suffolk (Fig. 5a) (which still survives), which was an advance in planning. It is polygonal in shape with three projecting rectangular turrets from which flanking fire could be directed along the whole face of the keep, and it also has a sloping base which was invaluable against mining. This was followed in 1185 by the circular keep at Conisborough Castle in Yorkshire (Fig. 5f), which has six solid wedge-shaped buttresses and a sloping base, so (as with Orford) when the defenders dropped missiles from above they would bounce off the slope at an enemy at an unpredictable angle. From this time the circular tower became popular, and by c.1200 a circular keep (now disappeared) had been erected on the motte of Egremont Castle. Circular keeps are fewer in number in England compared with the rectangular keep mainly because they came too late, as from the early 13th century the focus was on converting the bailey into the castle by heightening and thickening the curtain walls and providing them with circular angle and intermediate towers to give the defenders a wide range of fire. These towers became miniature keeps in themselves, each one blocking off a section of the wall so forcing an attacker to take each tower in turn in order to take the whole castle. In places a very strong gatehouse replaced the keep as the strong point, and in many cases the gatehouse was additionally strengthened with a barbican, an outwork which channelled and concentrated aggressors into the defender's line of fire. This change in planning allowed more space and thus comfort for living accommodation, and as we have seen with the keep, made many more mottes redundant. In some cases instead of building a keep as previously described, the palisade surrounding the summit of the motte was replaced by a circular or polygonal-shaped wall called a shell-keep (Fig. 6), against which lean-to buildings were erected around a small central courtyard (Fig. 6c). Usually as the shell-keep was erected the bailey was also enclosed with a wall which ascended two sides of the motte to join with the keep, in some cases concealing and protecting a stairway leading to the summit. There are no examples of this type of keep in Cumbria, but good examples elsewhere are Arundel (Sussex), Windsor (Berkshire), Pickering (Yorkshire), Totnes (Devon) and Launceston, Restormal and Trematon all in Cornwall (Fig. 6a, 6b and 6c). At Berkeley Castle (Gloucestershire) and Farnham Castle (Surrey), the walls of the shell-keep commence at the foot of the motte, acting as a revetment, and rise to enclose it completely.

Theoretically it had always been necessary to obtain the king's permission to build a castle, and William I had ordained that no defensive bank could be higher than 3m above the bottom of the ditch, that palisading on top of the bank could have no flanking salients, or elevated sentry walks, or outworks, and no castle could be built on any naturally isolated site like a rock or an island; he had also imposed restrictions on the construction of moats but this part of the law and that governing palisades was soon abandoned as unenforceable. Until the accession of Henry II in 1154 little was done to enforce the law but from this time permission was necessary and from c.1200 those who wished to build a castle or fortify an existing structure had to obtain from the king, for a small fee, a licence to crenellate. The licence allowed the applicant to build and crenellate a wall above a certain height and to add towers etc., and from c.mid-13th century the wording of the licence was basically as shown below:

'Licence for (name of applicant) and his heirs to enclose a place called (name of place and county), with a dyke (ditch and bank) and a wall of stone and lime and to crenellate it, and to hold it so fortified and crenellated forever'

and it usually ended with appropriate words giving the reason why it was granted (probably copied from the applicant's request), such as that added to the licence granted for Hartley Castle in 1353 which ended ' because it was situated near the Scottish March and has frequently in the past been burnt and destroyed by our enemies the Scots'. The licence was granted more or less automatically providing the applicant could afford to build and he was not openly hostile to the grantor, for it was not only the king who could issue them, but also the palatinates of Durham, Chester and after 1351, Lancaster. Licences were not only issued for building or rebuilding a castle, but also for fortifying a manor house, a town house, hospitals, parsonages, bishops' palaces, churches, the close of a cathedral and in one case, a belfry! Many of the northern nobles did not bother to apply for a licence, and that is why many of the fortified houses in the region called 'hall' or 'tower' not only look like a castle but are as strong or stronger than other buildings further south whose owners had been licensed. Sometimes those who built without permission merely received a mild rebuke and a retrospective licence, but at other times the king could be severe. A certain Berenger le Moyne built a castle without permission in 1266 at Barnwell in Northants, and when this fact was ascertained in 1276, he was forced to sell or give it and the lands attached to it to Ramsey Abbey. Hugh de Frene received a licence in 1292 for his manor-house at Moccas in Herefordshire which allowed him to 'strengthen it with a stone wall without tower or turret and not exceeding ten feet in height below the battlements', but he must have exceeded the limits for the castle was seized by the sheriff and though later restored to Hugh, it is probable that any excesses had been demolished.

Brougham Castle on the banks of the River Eamont.

By c.mid-14th century, with the exception of the Border areas, the licence was applied for more for prestige than necessity, and a number of those surviving castles built under licence from this period, have inadequately thin walls and/or poor defences. Between 1200 and 1570 about five hundred licences were granted, some of which were repeat licences, and of this total twenty were for sites in Cumbria. They are, in order of date, Kirkoswald 1201, Scaleby, Drumburgh and Dacre 1307, Brougham and Pendragon 1309, Wythop Hall 1318, Hayes 1322, Piel 1327, Naworth and Millom 1335, Rose 1336, Triermain 1340, Highhead 1342, Penrith town 1346, Wolsty 1348, Hartley and Greystoke 1353, Rose 1355 repeat, Workington Hall 1380, Penrith 1397 and again for Penrith 1399 which was an amended licence.

Under Edward I (1272-1307) the castle reached its zenith with the introduction of the concentric castles, first built between 1268-77 at Caerphilly in Glamorgan by Gilbert de Clare, Earl of Gloucester. The idea was seen and copied by Edward first at the Tower of London and then in his magnificent Welsh castles. The ultimate in concentricity can be seen in Fig. 7. After the death of Edward I in 1307 there began a decline in castles of

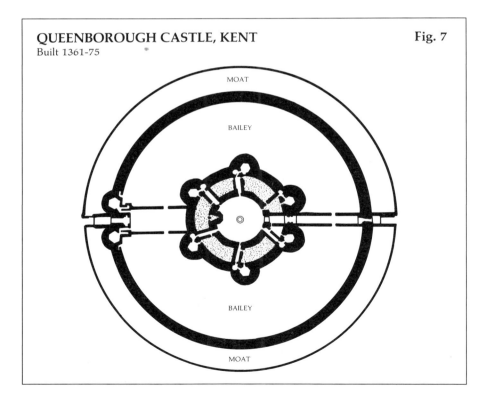

QUEENBOROUGH CASTLE, KENT   Fig. 7
Built 1361-75

MOAT

BAILEY

BAILEY

MOAT

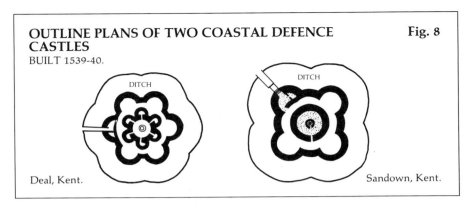

OUTLINE PLANS OF TWO COASTAL DEFENCE CASTLES

BUILT 1539-40.

DITCH

DITCH

Deal, Kent.

Sandown, Kent.

Fig. 8

a purely military nature, though of course many continued to be rebuilt, strengthened and adapted for the warfare of the day, but generally the trend was towards the fortified manor house which as the name implies, was comfortable to live in yet strong enough to withstand all but the most sustained attack. This can be illustrated by an event which took place in 1469 at Caister Castle, a brick-built fortified manor house in Norfolk which was besieged by the Duke of Norfolk with three thousand men, yet held out for several days before surrendering. These fortified manor houses, sometimes called 'castle' or sometimes 'hall', etc. were generally quadrangular in plan with a large rectangular entrance tower, usually in the centre of one side, smaller towers at the angles and surrounded by a moat.

The last castle built by the Crown for both residential and military reasons, was Queenborough Castle in Kent (Fig. 7), built between 1361-75, possibly to take the new artillery of the time, and can be compared with Henry VIII's coastal defence castles (Fig. 8). It had an uneventful life before its demolition in the early 17th century, and the only damage it sustained was caused not by warfare but by an act of God in 1382 when it was severely damaged by an earthquake! The final royal military 'castles' were really coastal artillery forts (Fig. 8), erected by Henry VIII (1509-47) along the south and east coasts against threatened invasion, and some remained occupied by the military until after 1945. During the 17th century Civil War many castles were refortified by both sides, some of them standing up remarkably well to the fire power of the day, but this was to be the cause of their downfall as the victors could not risk their use by an enemy again, so many that survived the cannon were deliberately destroyed. Some were only partly destroyed and were converted for residential use and are occupied to this day, but others not capable of conversion were sold by their owners for the value of their materials and have almost or completely disappeared.

Note

The inclusion of a site in this book does not necessarily imply that it is open to visitors (unless otherwise shown), and the majority are on private land where unannounced visits would probably be unwelcome. Before visiting any site it would be wise to ask permission first, and those marked 'OTV' (Open to Visitors) to enquire about opening times. When visiting country sites, please observe the Country Code.

Acknowledgements

I wish to express my thanks to the staff at the Carlisle City Library for all their assistance, in particular to Alex Alves, Michael Danes, John Foster, Pat Sanderson, Malcolm Wallace and Stephen White; also to Denis Perriam for his comments and corrections. Last, but not least, many thanks to my wife Jackie for her suggestions and for the many times she typed and corrected the manuscript.

The heading for each site in the gazetteer comprises:

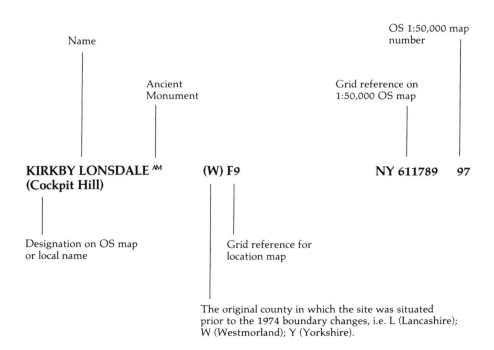

Name

OS 1:50,000 map number

Ancient Monument

Grid reference on 1:50,000 OS map

KIRKBY LONSDALE ᴬᴹ (Cockpit Hill)

(W) F9

NY 611789   97

Designation on OS map or local name

Grid reference for location map

The original county in which the site was situated prior to the 1974 boundary changes, i.e. L (Lancashire); W (Westmorland); Y (Yorkshire).

INDEX OF SITES

Main entries, with alternative names, are given in capitals. Names which only appear in the Appendix are given in lower case.

ABBEY FLATTS
Aikton   see Appendix
ALDINGHAM
APPLEBY
ARMATHWAITE
ASKERTON
ASPATRIA
Atterpile   see Castlehead
                          (Grange)
Augill   see Appendix
Averell   see Appendix
AYKERIST/
    AYKHURST   see Hayes

BEAUMONT
BECKERMET   see Caernarvon
Beetham Hall   see Appendix
BEWCASTLE/BELCASTLE
BEWLEY
Birch   see Appendix
BOA/BOTHE/BOWE   see Bewcastle
BRAMPTON
BRAYSTONES   see under
                          Caernarvon
BROOME   see Brougham
BROUGH
BROUGHAM/BROUHAM/BROWHAM
Brown   see Appendix
BRUHAM/BRUM   see Brougham
Buck   see Appendix
BULY   see Bewley
BURC/BURG/BURGH/
    BURGO   see Brough
BURGHAM   see Brougham
BURGH BY SANDS

CAERNARVON
CARLISLE
Carnick   see Waitby
Castelewyn   see Castle Hewin
Casteliadolf   see Castle Rock
Castelslac   see Castle Slack
Castelyadolfbek/
    Castelyndolf   see Castle Rock
Castilowe   see Appendix
Castle, The (Askham)   see Appendix
Castle, The (Coniston)   see Yewfield
Castle, The (Sawrey)   see Castlehill Wood
Castle Bank
    (Brampton)   see Appendix

Castle Bank
    (Grayrigg)   see Appendix
Castle Banks
    (Little Strickland)   see Appendix
Castleber   see Appendix
CASTLE CARROCK   and see Appendix
Castle Cleugh   see Appendix
Castle Colby   see Appendix
CASTLE CRAG
    (Bampton)
Castle Crag
    (Borrowdale)   see Appendix
Castle Crag
    (Kentmere)   see Appendix
Castle Crag
    (Wythburn)   see Appendix
Castle Crag   see Castle How
                          (Grasmere) and
                          Shoulthwaite
Castle Dubdale   see Appendix
Castledyke, Low   see Appendix
Castle Farm
    (Hardendale)   see Appendix
Castle Farm
    (Low Hesket)   see Appendix
Castle Farm
    (Near Sawrey)   see Castlehill Wood
Castle Fell   see Castle Bank
                          (Grayrigg)
Castlefield
    (Beckfoot)   see Appendix
Castlefield (Walton)   see Appendix
Castle Folds (Asby)   see Appendix
Castle Folds (Orton)   see Castle How
                          (Orton)
Castlegate   see Castle Crag
                          (Bampton)
Castle Gate
    (Watermillock)   see under Maiden
                          (Watermillock)
CASTLEHAW-HAUGH
Castle Head
    (Grange)   see Appendix
Castle Head
    (Keswick)   see Appendix
Castle Hewin   see Appendix
Castle Hill (Boothby)   see Appendix
Castle Hill
    (Cumwhitton)   see Appendix
Castle Hill (Dufton)   see Appendix

Castle Hill
   (Haresceugh)   see Haresceugh
Castle Hill
   (Kirklinton)   see Appendix
Castle Hill   see Castle Tower
CASTLE HILL (Warcop)
Castlehill Wood
   (Near Sawrey)   see Appendix
Castlehow
   (Ennerdale)   see Appendix
Castle How
   (Grasmere)   see Appendix
CASTLE HOW
   (Greenholme)   see under Tebay
Castle How
   (Harter Fell)   see Appendix
CASTLE HOW
   (Kendal)   see under Kendal
Castle How
   (Little Langdale)   see Appendix
Castle How
   (Old Hutton)   see Appendix
Castle How (Orton)   see Appendix
Castle How (Peel
   Wyke/Wythop)   see Appendix
Castlehow (Shap)   see Appendix
CASTLE HOW
   (Sowerby)   see Castle Sowerby
Castle How
   (Troutbeck)   see under High Cross
Castle How (Uldale)   see Appendix
Castle How (Ulpha)   see Appendix
CASTLE HOWE
   (Tebay)   see Tebay
Castlehowe Scar   see Castle Farm
             (Hardendale)
Castlehows Point
   (Watermillock)   see under Maiden
             (Watermillock)
Castle Knott
   (Middleton Fells)   see Appendix
Castle Luen   see Castle Hewin
Castlemont   see Aspatria
Castle Neb   see Appendix
Castle Nook   see Hardcastle
Castlerig   see Hayes
Castlerigg (Keswick)   see Castle Head
             (Keswick)
Castlerigg
   (Lazonby Fell)   see Appendix
Castle Rock   see Appendix
Castlescugh   see Castleskua
Castleshields   see Appendix
Castleside   see Castle, The
             (Askham)
Castleskua/
   Castleskews   see Appendix

Castle Slack   see Appendix
CASTLE SOWERBY
Castlesteads
   (Anthorn)   see Appendix
Castlesteads (Asby)   see Castle Folds
             (Asby)
Castlesteads
   (Dalston)   see Appendix
CASTLESTEADS
   (Lowther)   see under Lowther
Castlesteads
   (Natland)   see Appendix
Castlesteads
   (Pardshaw)   see Appendix
Castlesteads
   (Plumpton)   see Appendix
Castlesteads (Walton)   see Appendix
Castlesteads
   (Yanwath)   see Appendix
Castle Tower   see Appendix
Castling   see Appendix
Catcastle   see Appendix
CLIFTON
Cobra   see Appendix
COCKERMOUTH/
   COCKERMUE
Collinsons   see Appendix
CORBY
COUPLAND
CRAYSTOCK   see Greystoke
CREW
Crewgarth   see Castle Slack
             (Ouseby)
Croglam   see Appendix
CROSBY ON EDEN
CULGAITH/
   CULCHET

DACRE
DALTON IN FURNESS
Denton, Upper, and
   Denton Hall   see Appendix
DERWENTWATER
Dovenby Hall   see Appendix
DOWNHALL
Drawdykes   see Appendix
DRUMBURGH/DRUMBOGH
Dunmallet/
   Dunmallard   see Appendix
DUNMALLOGHT/
   DUNMALLOCK
Dunwalloght   see Appendix
DYKHURST   see Hayes

Edmond   see Appendix
EGREMONT/EGERMOND
Emount   see Edmond

Howgill Castle: basically an 18th-century rebuild of a late 14th-century towerhouse.

Drumburgh Castle, built c.1500 to guard the fords crossing the Solway Firth.

Forceknott — see Appendix
FOTHERAY, PIEL OF/
    FOULDREY — see Piel
Frizington — see Appendix

Gill — see Appendix
Glasson — see Lazon
GLEASTON/GLESTON
GRASTOKE — see Greystoke
Great Castle Howe — see Castle How
    (Grasmere)
Green — see Appendix
Greencastle — see Appendix
Greeny/Green — see Appendix
GREYSTOKE

Hallbankgate — see Appendix
HARCLA — see Hartley
Hardcastle — see Appendix
Hardknott — see Appendix
Haresceugh — see Appendix
HARTLEY
HAYES/HAY
HAYTON (Aspatria)
HAYTON (Brampton)
Headswood — see Appendix
HEGATCASTLE/HEHED/
    HEIGHHEVED — see Highhead
Heights — see Appendix
HEYHEVED — see Highhead
High Cross — see Appendix
HIGHED/HIGHENED/HIGHGATE/
    HIGHYATE — see Highhead
HIGHHEAD
HIGHYATE — see Highhead
HOLME CULTRAM
Hornby — see Appendix
How, The — see Appendix
HOWDALE — see under
    Kirkcambeck
HOWGILL — see also under
    Castle Sowerby
HYGHETT — see Highhead
Hyndcastell — see Appendix

Ing Castell — see Castle Rock
IRTHINGTON

KENDAL/KIRKBY-KENDAL
KIRKBY LONSDALE
KIRKCAMBECK
Kirklinton — see Castle Hill
    (Kirklinton)
KIRKOSWALD

LAMMERSIDE
Lamplugh — see Appendix

Lasen — see Lazon
LAUUEDRE — see Lowther
Laysin — see Lazon
Lazon/Lazen/Leyson — see Appendix
LAZONBY
LIDDEL STRENGTH/MOTE
LINSTOCK
Little Castle How — see Castle How
    (Grasmere)
LOWTHER — see also Appendix

Maborough — see Appendix
Maiden (Harter Fell) — see Castle How
    (Harter Fell)
Maiden (Lazonby Fell) — see Castlerigg
    (Lazonby Fell)
Maiden (Low Abbey) — see Appendix
Maiden (Stainmore) — see Appendix
Maiden (Wasdale) — see Appendix
Maiden (Watermillock/
    Soulby) — see Appendix
Maiden — see Braystones
MALLERSTANG/
    MALVESTANG — see Pendragon
MARYPORT
Mawbray — see Castlefield
    (Beckfoot)
Mayden — see Maiden
    (Stainmore) and
    (Watermillock)
MILLOM
Monk — see Appendix
MUCHLAND — see Gleaston
MUNCASTER — and see Monk
Mungo — see St Mungo's

NAWORTH
Newton — see Castlefield
    (Beckfoot)

Old (Glenridding) — see Appendix
Old (Triermain) — see Appendix
ORMSIDE, GREAT

PAB(P)CASTRE — see Papcastle
Palmcastel — see Appendix
PAPCASTLE — see under
    Cockermouth
PELE — see Piel
PENDRAGON
PENNINGTON — and see Appendix
PENRITH
PIEL
PIPARDS/PIPERS — see Papcastle
Plumpton — see Castlesteads
    (Plumpton)
Popes — see Appendix

Raby   see Appendix
Ratten   see Appendix
Rattenby   see Appendix
Reecastle   see Appendix
ROCKCLIFFE
ROCLIFFE/ROKELE   see Rockcliffe
ROOS   see Rose (Dalston)
Roper   see Appendix
ROSE (Dalston)
Rose (Hawkshead)   see Appendix
Ross   see Appendix
Round   see Castle Rock
ROWCLIFFE   see Rockcliffe

St Mungo's   see Appendix
Salkeld, Little   see Aikton
SCALEBY
Sebergham   see Appendix
SELBY   see Scaleby
SHANK
Shoulthwaite   see Appendix
SIZERGH
SKALBY   see Scaleby
SMARDALE
SOUREBI(Y)   see Castle Sowerby
Starling   see Appendix
Stonehaugh   see Appendix

Tarn   see Appendix
TEBAY
Toppin   see Appendix
TRADERMAYNE/TREVERMANE/
    TRIDERMAINE   see Triermain
TRIERMAIN
Triermain, Castle
    Rock of   see Castle Rock
TRIVERMAIN   see Triermain
Trostremont   see Dunmalloght and
                                  Castilowe
Typping   see Toppin

ULSTEY   see Wolsty

VLSTEY   see Wolsty

Waitby   see Appendix
Walls   see Appendix
WARCOP   see Castle Hill
                                  (Warcop)
Waw   see Walls
WELLOP/WELP   see Whelp
WESTNEWTON
WHEALLEP   see Whelp
WHELP
Whitehaven   see Appendix
WODOBANK   see under
                                  Caernarvon

WOLMSTY/
    WOOLSTEY   see Wolsty
WOLSTY
WORKINGTON HALL
Wray   see Appendix
WRISTIE   see Wolsty
WYRKYNGTON   see Workington Hall
WYTHOP/WYTHEHOPE

Yewfield   see Appendix
Yoadcastle   see Appendix

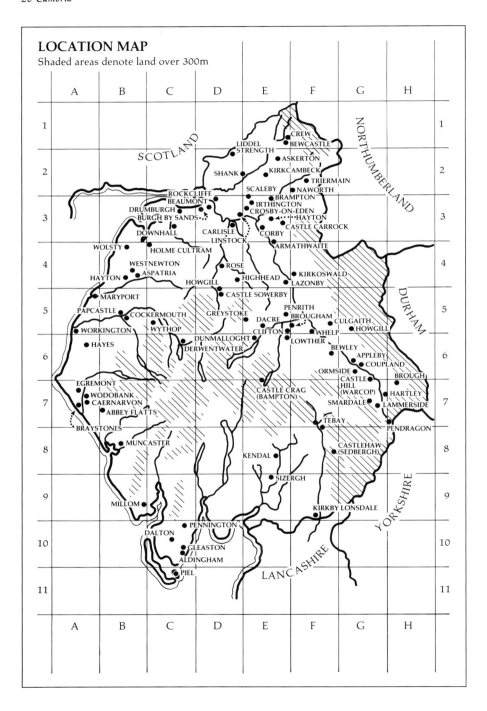

LOCATION MAP

Shaded areas denote land over 300m

GAZETTEER

ABBEY FLATTS B7 NY 052075 89

A possible motte and bailey formed from a natural mound called Flatts Cop situated on the summit of a hill ¼km N of Abbey Flatts Farm, 5¼km SE of EGREMONT. The motte has a summit diameter of c.30m, and the bailey, which lies to the W, is c.28m wide E-W.

ASC p.24

ALDINGHAM AM (L) C10 SD 278698 96/97
(Moat Hill)

A motte and bailey, its E side much damaged by erosion, situated on the edge of a steep cliff overlooking Morecambe Bay, 1km SSW of the village, 8km S of Ulverston. It comprises a motte at the southern end of what was probably intended to be a crescentic-shaped bailey, now indicated only by its N side ditch, c.6m wide.

The motte is 9.14m high above its surrounding ditch, which is 3m deep and 6m wide, and has base and summit diameters of c.61 and 31m respectively. Excavations in 1967 showed that an earlier ringwork was filled in and heightened 4m to form a motte, and at the same time the bailey was added. In the late 12c the motte was heightened and the bailey ditch widened and deepened, but for unknown reasons the work was not completed and in the first half of the 13c, possibly c.1227 when the rent and services of the le Flemings were transferred from the Crown to the Abbot of Furness, it was abandoned, probably in favour of a nearby moated site.

In 1102 the manor was confiscated from Roger the Poitevin who may have founded the ringwork, and c.1107 was granted to Michael le Fleming, who may have converted it into a motte, which was later heightened, possibly by his descendants.

AF pp.388-91; T.9(1880)pp.409-11, 6(1906)pp.320-1, 24(1924)pp.260-5, 271-7; BN.3(1880-2)p.119; VCH(L)2pp.556-8; CT pp.34-6, 142; MA.13(1969)pp.258-9; OS.SD26NE/2.

APPLEBY Parts AM (W) G6 NY 685199 91

It stands on a headland in the town and comprises the masonry castle, originally either a ringwork and bailey or motte and bailey enclosed by a much rebuilt 12c curtain wall. The ringwork or motte was later adapted into an inner bailey, 49m in diameter, and contains the keep, the remainder forming an outer bailey, 70 x 52m, containing the domestic buildings. To the NW are remains of a crescent-shaped outer enclosure (1) 64 x 128m, containing 17c stables (2) and

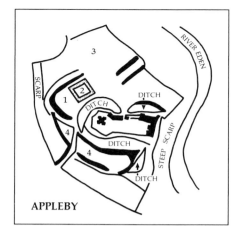

APPLEBY

two southern angles contain circular stairways giving access to the upper floors and roof, that on the SE also giving access to the ground floor. There are two entrances, both on the E side, that at first floor level being the original. During 17c conversions a floor was removed and an E-W cross-wall added.

The outer bailey contains the mainly two-storey residential buildings which date from the 15c to the 17c with later alterations, but also incorporate some 12c work at the eastern end. There are rectangular towers at the eastern angles (5), a circular one projecting from the N side (6), and traces of a similar one of 13c date on the S side (7).

there are other enclosures: to the N (3) 49 x 122m, and to the SW (4) 28 x 174m. The castle dates from the 12c but has been much modernised and restored: the keep is a museum, and the outer enclosures have been adapted for use as a wildlife park.

The three storey keep, built c.1170, is 14.17m square over walls 1.83m thick and 24.38m high to the top of the angle turrets, the latter being later additions to the shallow clasping buttresses. The walls were heightened during the 13c and the original level is still visible. The

The castle was founded between 1100-20 by Ranulph le Meschin (died c.1129) and apparently passed to the Crown in 1120-21 when Ranulph succeeded to his cousin's earldom of Chester. In 1136 it was ceded to the Scots who held it until 1157 when it reverted to the Crown, and was immediately granted to Hugh de Morville (died 1202) who probably built the keep. It was confiscated in 1173 and in 1179 granted to Theobald de Valoines, reverting to the Crown from 1190 until 1203 when it

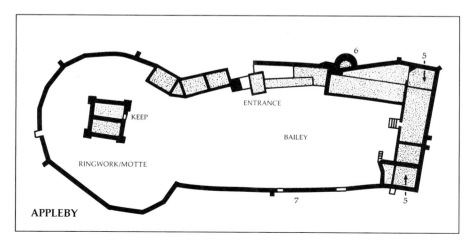

APPLEBY

was granted to Robert de Vipont, nephew of Hugh de Morville, and allowed to decay. In 1269 it passed by marriage to Roger de Clifford (drowned 1282) whose descendants in their 400-year tenure (except for a period of confiscation between 1461-85), restored it and made many improvements. It was rebuilt c.1454 by Thomas, Lord Clifford, but was probably damaged between 1461-85 and was described as 'ruinous' in c.1539 though still used as a gaol. In 1569 it was slighted by Henry Clifford, 2nd Earl of Cumberland (died 1570) 'so as to be of no use to anyone should it be taken', and was further damaged during the Civil War, remaining ruinous until 1651 when it was rebuilt by Anne Clifford, Countess of Pembroke (died 1676). After her death it passed by marriage to Thomas Tufton, Earl of Thanet (died 1729) who made many alterations between 1686-8, including doubling the width of the N wing and facing it with masonry from BROUGH and BROUGHAM castles. It was sold by descendants to a private company c.1950. Occupied. OTV. GA.

T.1(1866-73)pp.242-54, 8(1885)pp.382-95, 49(1949)pp.118-33; OMH pp.27-30; CE.2 pp.280-1; CT pp.66-7, 75-80, 454; RC pp.7-13; CL.87(1940)pp.382-6, 408-12; HKW.2 p.553; CCW pp.29-31; OS.NY61NE/1.

ARMATHWAITE   E4   NY 505459   86

A late 16c or early 17c mansion, measuring 21.64 x 14.33m with later alterations and additions, and incorporating a probable mid-15c towerhouse, 15.85 x 8.23m, in the SW angle. It stands S of the village on the W bank of the River Eden, 14½km SE of CARLISLE.

The tower is attributed to John Skelton (died c.1458), who was granted land here by the king in 1444, but was first mentioned between 1509-47. The tower was probably incorporated into the mansion in the late 16c or the early 17c, and was sold in 1712 to the Sandersons who held it until 1741 and made some alterations and additions. In 1741 it passed by marriage to the Milbournes who by c.1802 had 'modernised' it, and it was sold to the Earl of Lonsdale in 1846. It was later acquired by the Ackroyds and was purchased by the Armstrongs c.1949 who converted it into flats. It has since reverted back to a private dwelling. Occupied.

T.8(1886)pp.382-95, 13(1913)p.343, 23(1923)pp.39-40; CE.2 p.295; CT p.343; BE p.61; CCW p.32; Armathwaite Castle, the Building and its History. D. Perriam (Title forthcoming); OS.NY54NW/14.

ASKERTON   E2   NY 551692   86

This much restored castle, measuring 26 x 23m, now a farmhouse, stands on a spur of high ground situated 8km NNE of BRAMPTON.

The main block, a fortified house, 7.93 x 18.29m over walls c.1.12m thick, was built c.1478 but has been much altered, the doorways and windows

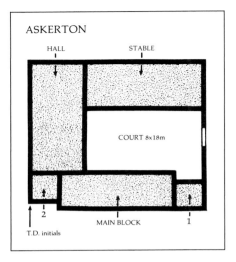

ASKERTON

HALL   STABLE

COURT 8x18m

MAIN BLOCK

2

1

T.D. initials

being late 19c insertions added when the floor levels were altered. The angle towers were added c.1500 and positioned so that both sides of the house could be overlooked: the 'Dovecot Tower' (1) 3.35 x 4.57m, overlooking the N front, is set back 3.35m and blocks the original entrance, and the 'Dacre Tower' (2) 3.66 x 6.10m, overlooking the S front, is set back 1.53m. Both of the recesses formed by the siting of these towers are corbelled across the angles and contain garderobe chutes. The hall, 7.32 x 15.24m and the stable block, 7.62 x 19.20m, were added between 1500-25, the latter probably having barrack accommodation above. The hall has lost its battlements but retains part of a staircase which gave access to them.

Between 1500-25 the fortified house was incorporated into an extensive re-modelling carried out by Thomas, Lord Dacre, Warden of the West March, whose initials can be seen on the weather moulding of the 'Dacre Tower'. Because of the Dacres' participation in the 1569

rebellion, the castle was forfeited and partially dismantled, and between 1576-98 was occupied by Thomas Carleton, a land-sergeant, who let it go to ruin, a survey of 1589 recording it as 'in very great decay'. In August 1598 it was granted to John Musgrave who immediately set about its repair and in the November of that year 'Askerton house and castle' was described as 'a house of good strength and defence, and the only house in Gilsland fit for the Land Sergeant [the Warden's officer] to dwell in'. It passed by marriage to the Howards who eventually gained possession in 1601 after paying Queen Elizabeth I c.£10,000 'to redeem their possessions' which also included NAWORTH castle, etc. It was modernised during the later 19c and restored in 1922. Occupied.

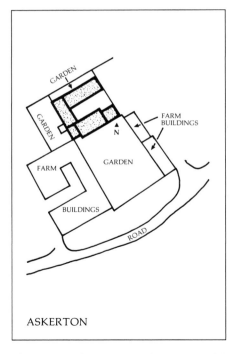

GARDEN

GARDEN

GARDEN

FARM
BUILDINGS

N

FARM

GARDEN

BUILDINGS

ROAD

ASKERTON

T.3(1876-7)pp.178-81, 11(1911)pp.254-8, 24(1924)pp.149-55; OMH p.350; CE.2 p.296; CT pp.344-6; BCP p.28; CCW pp.33-5; OS.NY56NE/1.

ASPATRIA   B4   NY 134415   85
(Castlemont)

Castlemont, a modern house situated on high ground 1km W of the town, reputedly occupies the site of 'Aspatria Castle', traditionally founded by Gospatrick (died c.1075), Lord of this district at the time of the Norman Conquest.

The house overlies an early settlement, and immediately S are traces of a circular univallate enclosure. A nearby field is called both 'Castlesteads' and 'Hallsteads'.

EB p.134; Arch. J. 132(1975)p.31; OS.NY14SW/13.

BEAUMONT   D3   NY 348592   85

A much damaged motte and bailey situated in the centre of the village, 6¼km NW of CARLISLE, the motte wholly occupied by the church (which contains some 12c work) and the churchyard. It is built on the line of Hadrians Wall, and the motte covers the site of Roman Milecastle 70A.

The oval shaped motte is c.4m high with base and summit diameters of 43 x 49m and 28 x 37m respectively. The bailey, 46 x 55m, which lay to the NE and until the mid 19c was called 'Castle Green', has been built over.

It was probably founded in the 12c by the le Bruns 'often called de Feritate - i.e. of the waste', and passed on the death of Robert de la Ferte (died 1300) to his cousin, Richard le Brun. It was possibly abandoned by Richard's grandson, Robert, who received a licence to crenellate for DRUMBURGH in 1307, though part of it may have remained in use as a dower house until c.1380.

SRW p.80; CT p.38; RW pp.212-3; CFH p.44; OS.NY35NW/27.

BEWCASTLE ^{AM}   E1   NY 565748   86
or BELCASTELL, BOA, BOTHE, BOWE

This ruinous castle stands on a mound in the NE angle of a Roman fort immediately N of the church, 24km NE of CARLISLE. The mound, c.3m high, was formed by isolating the angle of the fort with an L-shaped ditch and throwing the material inwards to heighten it. The castle was quadrangular, c.27m square over walls 2m thick, at base, with a gatehouse and barbican, c.7.32 x 10.06m, probably added c.1470, projec-

ting from the W side. The S wall of the castle, c.9m high, survives almost to its full original height, and at first-floor level has remains of two chimney flues and two blocked Tudor period windows. Parts of the other walls survive and the interior, probably originally having lean-to buildings around a small courtyard, is filled with grass-covered mounds of fallen masonry. The gatehouse, c.7.32m square, contains a flight of steps in the

W wall ascending to a short passage and garderobe in the S wall, the passage wall containing two 'spy-holes' over-looking the interior. A portion of the W wall extending beyond the entrance is all that remains of a barbican added in the 16c.

The castle was reputedly founded c.1092 by Bueth, a Saxon or Danish chieftain who must have been an adherent of the Normans, as otherwise it is unlikely that he would have been allowed to erect and occupy a castle. It is more probable that it was founded by William II, and handed over to Bueth once he had proved trustworthy, and was prob-ably confiscated from Bueth's grandson Robert, who fought with the Scots in 1174. Before 1210 the manor had been acquired by the de Levingtons, and was purchased c.1271-77 by John de Swinburne, sheriff of Cumberland, who may have rebuilt the castle with masonry. It was confiscated in 1296 from Adam de Swinburne (died c.1327) because of his adherence to John Balliol but was later restored to him and c.1327 passed by marriage to John de Strivelyn, Constable of Edinburgh Castle.

The first reference to a castle here was after John de Strivelyn's death in 1378 and a keystone bearing his coat of arms, reputedly once above the castle entrance, is now set into the wall of an adjacent farm building. In 1391 it passed to the de Middletons, who allowed it to decay, and by 1470 when it was granted to Richard, Duke of Gloucester, both castle and manor had been 'long lying waste'. Richard, as Warden of the West March, is thought to have repaired the castle and also to have added the gate-house, but it is possible that the gate-house was added during the Tudor period, possibly after 1517 when a plan

to demolish the castle and replace it with a new one at Arthuret, 15km WSW, was abandoned. In 1541-2 repairs were made which included deepening the ditches and the addition of a bar-bican, an extra £40 being allocated for its completion later in 1542. Its demise began c.1550, and a survey made in 1565 records that the barmekin wall was 'utterly decayed, the ditches filled with earth and mud, whereby men and cattle may pass in and fourth', and there was a breach, 15.24m wide, in the N wall. The estimated cost of repairs, £320, was evidently too much and the castle was more or less abandoned. In 1614 the manor and castle were leased to the Earl of Cumberland, but in 1629 both were granted to the Grahams of Netherby who held them into the 20c. For a short time in 1639 the ruins were garrisoned by 100 men, and it was reputedly slighted by them on their departure, but there is a local tradition that it was destroyed by a Parliamentary battery sited at 'Cannon Holes', an earthwork a short distance to the E, and cannonballs have been found in and

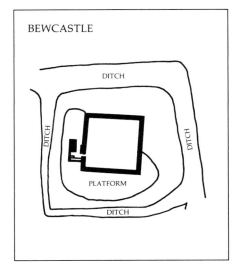

BEWCASTLE

DITCH

DITCH

DITCH

PLATFORM

DITCH

around the castle. It was sold in 1968 to a London-based property company who intended to sell portions of it to the Americans, but the plan fell through.

OMH pp.346-9; CE.2 pp.296-7; T.11(1911)pp.244-50, 22(1922) pp.186-97, 29(1929)pp.63-8; CT pp.138-41, 497-9; Cumberland News 31.5.1968; BCP pp.41-2; CCW pp.38-40; HKW 3 pt.1 pp.233-4, 403; CFH pp.45, 328, 330-1; OS.NY57SE/4.

BEWLEY ᴬᴹ (W) F6 NY 648212 91

The ruins of what was more a fortified manor house than a castle stand adjacent to Old Bewley Farm at the end of a track, 2¼km SW of APPLEBY. They comprise a main N-S block, 19.51 x 8.53m over walls 1.22m-1.52m thick, with a garderobe turret (1) 3 x 3.66m, projecting from the SW angle, and a tower (2) 5.49 x 5.79m also with a garderobe turret (3), at the SE angle. There are traces of adjoining buildings to the N and W.

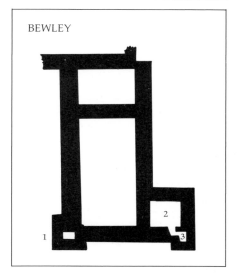

BEWLEY

The original building here was probably founded by Bishop Hugh de Beaulieu of Carlisle (1219-23), but there are no remains of this period as it was probably demolished c.1325 when the present building was erected by Bishop John Ross (1325-32). Restoration work in 1402 by Bishop William Strickland (1400-19), included re-roofing the chapel and the 'lord's chamber', and later in the 15c it was leased to the Machel family who lived here until the early 18c. It probably fell into decay about this time and in 1774, when held by the Musgraves, it was described as 'a mean ruinous building', though by 1789 the walls still stood almost to their full original height. It was sold by the Church Commissioners in 1857 and gradually reduced to the ruin we see today. A church service is usually held here on Rogation Sunday.

T.8(1886)pp.413-5, 461, 3(1903)pp.240-62, 27(1927)pp.184-8; OMH pp.119-22; CE.2 p.285; CT pp.253-4; RC pp.43-4; CCW pp.40-1; OS.NY62SW/1.

BRAMPTON ᴬᴹ E3 NY 532612 86
(The Mote)

A motte formed from the summit of Castle Hill with a possible bailey to the N, situated on the E side of the town. It was used as a beacon by at least 1468.

The motte has an oval-shaped summit, 38 x 14m, with traces of a breastwork, and is isolated on the N side by a ditch, c.7m wide and 3m deep, with an outer bank c.1m high. The possible bailey is indicated by a roughly kidney-shaped platform.

T.5(1905)p.290; CT p.39; OS.NY56SW/1.

BROUGH ᴬᴹ   (W) H7   NY 791141   91

Between 1174 and 1202 it was called BURC, BURG, BURGH and BURGO. The castle, originally either a motte and bailey or ringwork and bailey, occupies the N half of a Roman fort situated on high ground S of the village, 13km SE of APPLEBY, and is surrounded by a ditch, c.2.44m deep and 18m wide.

It is roughly triangular, 87m E-W x 43m and 18m N-S at the E and W ends respectively. The three-storey 13-15c gatehouse (1) in the S curtain gives access to a large courtyard with foundations of the main domestic buildings of c.1380 (2) to the right and those of the stables (3) to the left, and opposite in the NE angle are remains of 17c domestic buildings (4) which include a brewery and a kitchen. The W end of the courtyard is mainly taken up by the keep (5). The circular 'Clifford Tower', 9.14m in diameter (6), probably of 13c date but reconstructed in the 17c, projects from the SE angle.

The three-storey keep, 15.55 x 12.50m, over walls 3.05m thick at base reducing to c.1.83m above, is c.18m high, with clasping angle buttresses rising above the roof to form rectangular turrets, three of which survive. The lower stages of the keep date from c.1170, and the remainder from after 1174. Excavations in 1925 showed that the keep was built over a rectangular tower of c.1100, possibly the original keep. Most of the E side has long been

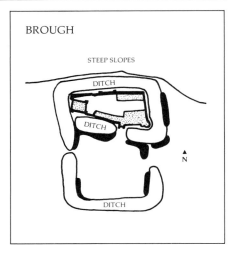

BROUGH

STEEP SLOPES

DITCH

DITCH

N

DITCH

destroyed, and the SW angle 'crashed to the ground - causing a breach in the wall from 15 to 18 feet wide' on the morning of May 29th, 1920.

The original castle, built c.1093 by William II, was ceded to the Scots in 1136 who held it until 1157 when it reverted to the English Crown and was immediately granted to Hugh de Morville (died 1202) to whom the keep is generally attributed. Confiscated in 1173, it was almost totally destroyed by the Scots in 1174, and in 1179 was granted to Theobald de Valoines who probably heightened or rebuilt the keep. It was confiscated again in 1190 and held by the Crown until 1203 when it was granted to Robert de Vipont,

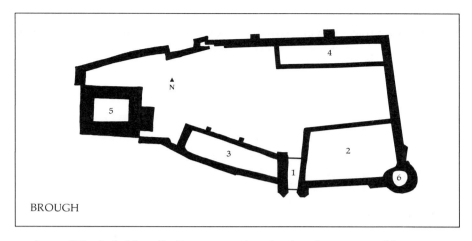

BROUGH

nephew of Hugh de Morville. In 1269 it passed by marriage to the Cliffords who rebuilt and added to it, and it apparently remained occupied until 1521 when it was 'set on fire by casual mischance - and it long remained waste - going to utter ruin more and more'. Between 1660-61 it was restored and made habitable by Anne Clifford, Countess of Pembroke (died 1676), but after her death, when it passed by marriage to the Tuftons, earls of Thanet, it was allowed to decay, and in 1695 materials were removed for use at APPLEBY castle. The fittings were sold in 1714, and c.1763 part of the 'Clifford Tower' was demolished. In 1928 it was presented to the predecessors of EH by Lord Hothfield, a descendant of the Tuftons. OTV. GA.

T.6(1881-2)pp.26-7, 9(1909)pp.177-91, 27(1927)pp.224-7, 46(1946)pp.223-83; MMA.1 pp. 286-94; OMH pp.31-3; CE.2 p.282; CT pp.66-7, 81-6; RC pp.50-3; HKW.2 p.582; NCB pp.118-20; CCW pp.44-7; OS.NY71SE/1.

BROUGHAM ᴬᴹ   (W) F5   NY 538289   90
or BROOME, BROUHAM, BROWHAM, BRUHAM, BRUM, BURGHAM

The substantial red sandstone remains dating mainly from the 13c. and 14c. stand on the S bank of the River Eamont, near its confluence with the River Lowther, 2¼km ESE of PEN-RITH. It adjoins the Roman fort of Brocavum, the N ditch of which, c.17m wide, has been extended around the E and W sides of the castle into the old bed of the Lowther. The mainly 13c curtain wall, up to 9.14m high and 1.52m thick, encloses an irregular shaped area, 71m N-S x 73m SW-NE x 57m E-W at the N end. The entrance is at the NE angle through an outer gate (1) added c.1300, and an inner gate (2) of c.1290. Opposite the inner gate is the keep (3), with the hall (4) and other domestic buildings forming an L-shaped block along the E and S sides. There are foundations of buildings against the W wall and the rectangular 'Tower of League' (5) 7.62m x 8.84m projects from the SW angle. The keep, 13.41m square, built c.1170-

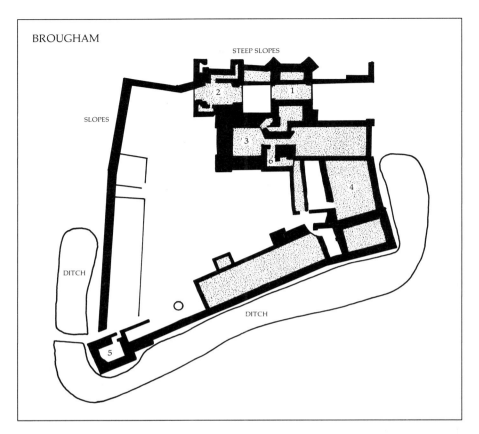

BROUGHAM

80, with a top storey added in the late 13c, has walls 3.35m thick at base reducing to 3.05m above, with a spiral stair in the NE angle giving access to all floors. A fore-building (6) c.9.14 x 6.10m projects from the E side.

The castle was probably founded soon after 1157 by Hugh de Morville (died 1202), though it was not mentioned in 1173 when the manor was forfeited, and was first recorded c.1228 after the death of Hugh's nephew, Robert de Vipont, who had been granted the manor in 1203. By 1245 it was 'in decay' remaining so until after 1269 when it passed by marriage to the Cliffords, and was probably rebuilt by Robert de

Clifford who received a licence to crenellate for 'Brouham' in 1309.

Later in the century there were many Scottish raids in the area and as a result the castle suffered much damage. In 1403 it was described as being 'worth nothing - it lieth waste by reason of the destruction of the Scots'. Between c.1550-70 it was restored by Henry Clifford, 2nd Earl of Cumberland (died 1570), and was visited by both James I and Charles I in 1607 and 1629 respectively, and it remained occupied until its slighting by Parliament in 1648.

Described c.1660 as 'Very ruinous and much out of repair' it was restored by Anne Clifford, Countess of

Pembroke, who lived here until her death in 1676. It passed to the Tuftons, earls of Thanet, and c.1695, the sixth earl removed materials for use at APPLEBY. The fittings were sold in 1714 and by 1767 the keep, the only habitable building, was occupied by a steward. The castle was presented to the EH predecessors by Lord Hothfield in 1928. OTV. GA.

T.1(1866-73)pp.66-70, 6(1881-2)pp.15-26, 22(1922)pp.143-57, 42(1942)pp.170-9, 76(1976)pp.67-76; DAE.2 pp.220-22; The Builder 34(1876)pp.683-6; MMA.1 pp.294-304; OMH pp.35-8; CE.2 pp.283-5; CT pp.66-7, 87-94, 454; Archaeologia 58(1903)pp.359-82; RC pp.55, 57-62; NCB pp.120-1, 123; CCW pp.47-52; HLC p.2; ASLD pp.64-75; OS.NY52NW/5.

BURGH BY SANDS   D3   NY 314592   85

There are no visible remains of this castle which occupied a low lying site W of the village, 9km WNW of CARLISLE. Excavations in 1950 revealed four building periods prior to its destruction in the 14c.

The first period, c.1100, comprised a motte with surrounding ditch, probably founded by Robert de Trevers, which later in the century was levelled and a grange surrounded by a rectangular shaped ditch built over it. Towards the end of the century, masonry buildings and a curtain wall were erected. Most of the buildings were demolished c.mid-13c and replaced by a fortified manor house comprising a rectangular block, c.10.36m x 15.55m, with a circular tower, c.7.62m in diameter, projecting from the NW angle, and a walled courtyard c.5m x 6m on the S side.

In c.1120 the castle passed by marriage from the de Trevers family to Ranulph Engaine, and after the death of his son William c.1158, it passed again by marriage to Simon de Morville (died 1167). After the death of Simon's son, Hugh, in 1202, it passed by marriage first to Richard de Lucy of EGREMONT (died 1213), and then to Thomas de Multon of Moulton in Lincolnshire, remaining with his descendants until c.1313. It passed by marriage to Ranulph Dacre (died 1339) and c.1314 was described as 'a capital messuage worth 24 shillings', but it was probably destroyed later by the Scots, for in 1362 it was described as 'a ruin worth nothing'. The ruins were visible until at least 1610, possibly until 1620 when 'Old Castle' was a field name here.

T.11(1911)pp.242-4, 54(1954)pp.105-30; CT p.20; EB pp.23-4; OS.NY35NW/6.

CAERNARVON   A7   NY 02.07.   89

There are three castle sites in the area. WODOBANK and BRAYSTONES are within 1½km of CAERNARVON CASTLE.

CAERNARVON CASTLE 021072

It was probably ploughed down before 1671 and now only faint earthworks are visible, situated on high ground ¼km NE of Beckermet, 3km SSE of

EGREMONT. Remains indicate a rectangular univallate enclosure, c.92 x 77m, with entrance gaps in the W and E sides, and a ditch 11m wide, originally c.3.66m deep. Two possibly associated natural mounds outside the enclosure were levelled c.1900: one of them, 'Coneygarth Cop' opposite the W entrance, was c.11m high and its summit c.5.50m in diameter. Excavations inside the enclosure in 1962 revealed evidence of a form of palisading, and 1m below the surface, just N of the site of Coneygarth Cop, a cobbled area was found.

The le Flemings were granted land here by William I, and possibly had their first residence at WODOBANK (below), abandoning it later in favour of this site. Richard le Fleming (died c.1207) was styled 'of Caernarvon Castle, Beckermet', and it probably remained in use until c.1250 when the family moved to Coniston. The Cumbrian meaning of 'Caenarvon' is 'the castle over against Mona' (the Isle of Man).

T.3(1903)pp.214-22; CT pp.21-2; OS.NY00NW/13.

WODOBANK 010081   A7

A motte and a possible bailey situated on high ground beside a dismantled railway which has destroyed the motte's NE side, 1½km NW of CAERNARVON castle. It consists of the motte, c.4m high, with base and summit diameters of c.22 and 9.14m respectively and traces of a possible kidney-shaped bailey to the W, c.33 x 16m. The eastern side of the motte is revetted with a 19c wall.

CT p.38; ASC p.23; OS.NY00NW/8.

BRAYSTONES
(Brough Hill) 009058   A7

A possible motte and bailey situated on the S bank of the River Ehen, 1½km SW of CAERNARVON castle. It comprises a roughly oval-shaped hill c.6m-9m high and measuring c.85 x 38m, with a late 19c tower occupying the site of the motte at the higher eastern end. It was possibly founded by the de Braithestones who held land here from the 12c until c.1390. Maiden Castle and Castlebank are parish field names.

GD p.153; CT p.39; BE p.66; PNC.2 p.414.

CARLISLE ^{Parts AM}   D3   NY 395564   85

The castle, possibly originally a ringwork and bailey, occupies the end of a steep-sided ridge rising gently from the S, on which side it was originally isolated from adjoining ground by two massive E-W cross-ditches of which the inner remains. The curtain wall, c.6.10m high and 3m thick encloses an area c.229m E-W x 122m N-S, the W and E curtains originally joining with the city walls at the outer ditch. The outer bailey, added c.1168 and now c.1.52m higher than its original level is entered through a gatehouse (1) in the S side, and contains

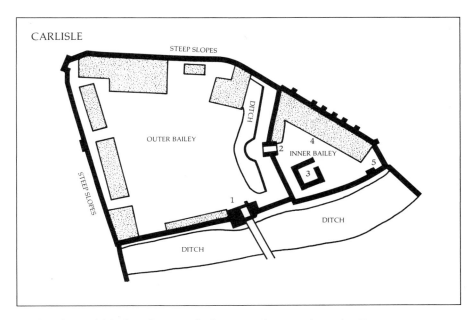

CARLISLE

STEEP SLOPES

DITCH

OUTER BAILEY

INNER BAILEY

STEEP SLOPES

DITCH

DITCH

modern barrack blocks. The inner bailey, c.76 x 61m, is isolated from the outer bailey by a N-S curtain wall with a gatehouse (2) and a ditch. It contains the keep (3) 18.29 x 21.42m and c.20m high, probably erected before 1175, but which has since undergone extensive alterations. The present entrance at ground floor level replaced the original which was to the first floor through a fore-building. The former magazine (4), now a museum, stands against the N wall with remains of the 14c 'Queen Mary's Tower' (5) demolished c.1835, at the SE angle.

The castle, founded c.1093 by William II, was ordered to be rebuilt by Henry I in 1122, and in 1135 was ceded to the Scots. It was probably rebuilt with masonry by King David, and after its surrender to Henry II in 1157 it remained a Crown possession. Between 1173-1461 it was besieged nine times by the Scots but only taken once, in 1216 by King Alexander II who repaired

and strengthened it. By 1255 it was in a ruinous condition but still garrisoned and apparently remained so, except for minor repairs, until 1542 when extensive repairs were made and the walls adapted to carry artillery. By 1563 the castle was in great decay and c.21m of the outer curtain wall, which had collapsed in 1557, had still not been rebuilt, but repairs were made and in 1568 Mary, Queen of Scots was held here for almost two months.

From October 1644 until June 1645 the castle and city were besieged by Parliamentary forces, and after the surrender the castle was garrisoned by the Scots until 1646. In 1648 it was surprised and taken by the Royalists but soon surrendered, and was next taken in November 1745 by the Jacobites who found it ruinous and held by 'two companies of invalids, some 80 in number, all old and infirm men'. The Scots were ejected in the following month by the Duke of Cumberland who caused

Appleby Castle: the 12th-century keep.

much damage to the castle by cannon. The castle was extensively 'modernised' in the 19c. EH. OTV. GA.

GM.7 pt.2(1859)pp.247-50; T.2(1874-5)pp.56-95, 18(1918)pp.235-7, 19(1919)pp.165-7; MMA.1 pp.350-8; CE.2 pp.297-302; ENC pp.123-5; CT pp.95-110; CG.3(1969)p.112; BCP pp.53-6; NCB pp.132-4; CCW pp.55-60; HKW.2 pp.595-600, 4 pt.2 pp.664-73; Ancient Monuments and their Interpretation (various authors) (1977)pp.191-200; ASLD pp.52-7; Carlisle Castle, forthcoming.

CASTLE CARROCK   E3   NY 544554   86

The castle site is unknown but is generally considered to be the moated site situated immediately E of the church. It measures c.92 x 46m with remains of a surrounding moat up to 6m wide and 0.61m deep, and traces of a possible fish pond to the SE. There is a local tradition that the castle stood on high ground immediately E of the moat and that masonry was dug up and removed 'many years ago'. On Jacobs Hill, situated NNE of the church, at GR 544556 are traces of a circular earthwork, c.52m in diameter internally, with a low, much spread bank.

The castle may have been founded by Gamel de Castlecarrock who is mentioned between 1160-70, and may have continued to be occupied until late in the reign of Edward I when the male line of the family became extinct. Masonry from the castle was reputedly used to build the predecessor to the present church. See also in the Appendix.

T.6(1881-2)p.465, 8(1908)pp.248-52; CFH p.58; OS.NY55NW/7.

CASTLE CRAG [AM]   (W) E7   NY 469128   90
(Bampton)

A probable ringwork and bailey formed from the summit of Castle Crag 412m above sea level, situated 7km SW of Bampton. It overlooked the road from Mardale village (both now covered by Haweswater Reservoir) to Bampton, and 'Castlegate' (i.e. 'Castle Road') mentioned in 1265 may refer to both the castle and the road. Castle Crag consists of a roughly oval-shaped ringwork formed from the NE end of the crag, separated from a roughly kidney-shaped bailey to the SW by a rock-cut ditch, 3.05m deep and 8.53m wide, and isolated from adjoining ground to the SW by another rock-cut ditch, 3.05m deep and 12.50m wide. The interior of the ringwork, c.14 x 8m, is enclosed by a breastwork, c.0.91m to 3.35m high, and 5.49m high above the ditch. It is at its highest and most massive on the bailey side, and at its SE end, overlooking the reservoir, it opens out to form an oval-shaped platform, c.7m in diameter. The entrance is from the inner ditch at the northern end. The bailey, c.15 x 7m, has the appearance of being unfinished. Excavations of the ringwork in 1922 though finding no datable objects, did reveal 'a parapet rampart on the northern side, built up to perpendicular height of 10 ft. from the under edge of the brow of the precipice', which was made up of 'tightly laid flat stones without any distinct facing'.

The site has no known history but it may have been built by the barons of Kendal both for use as a hunting lodge and to guard against intruders who might come via High Street, a Roman road along the top of nearby mountains.

T.23(1923)pp.285-6; RC pp.31-2; PNW.2 p.194; CG.3(1969)p.122; OS.NY41SE/1.

CASTLEHAW ᴬᴹ   (Y) F8   SD 662923   98
or CASTLEHAUGH

A damaged motte and bailey formed from the summit of a steep hill E of Sedbergh, 15km E of KENDAL. It comprises a circular motte with a U-shaped bailey to the W, c.23 x 30m. The motte is 8m high with base and summit diameters of c.35 and 3.35m respectively, the latter much reduced in size and built upon. It was surrounded by a ditch, c.5m wide, which opened out into the steep hillside to the S.

It was possibly founded by Robert de Mowbray, Earl of Northumberland, and perhaps demolished in 1095 when, because of his rebellion he was deprived of his earldom and his lands confiscated.

VCH(Y)2 p.37; OS.SD69SE/1.

CASTLE HILL   (W) G7   NY 750154   91
(Warcop)

There are no visible remains of this castle which stood in the village on Castle Hill, close to the cemetery, 4km WNW of BROUGH. Remains visible in the late 17c had disappeared before c.1777 when it was recorded that 'About 100 yards [92m] south-east from the village - was a castle which appears to have been a large building, and to have taken up more than one acre of ground. Mr Machel [a 17c antiquary] says that he had seen some part of the walls dug up, which were 15 foot thick, and of fair hewn stone, well cemented with lime and sand'.

It was probably founded by the de Warcops, who were here before 1228, but had been abandoned before c.1506 when by tradition, stones from the castle were taken to rebuild the tower of Kirkby Stephen church.

NB.1 p.606; T.4(1878-9)p.229 note; HKS p.36; OS.NY71NE/1.

CASTLE SOWERBY   D5   NY 36.38.   90

There were two sites here situated 1½km apart, CASTLE HOW and HOWGILL, but that at HOWGILL, possibly abandoned in favour of CASTLE HOW, has disappeared. Both have been suggested as the possible site of the 'castellum de Sourebi' mentioned in 1186-7.

The impressive motte and bailey called Castle How at Tebay.

Beaumont church stands on a fine motte.

Pendragon Castle, reputed to be the place where Uther Pendragon died.

CASTLE HOW 360383

A possible motte and bailey, perhaps adapted from a hill-fort, situated on the summit of a ridge on the W side of Castle Sowerby parish, 18km SSW of CARLISLE. It comprises a motte at the S end of the ridge, isolated from the bailey to the N by a rock-cut ditch which surrounds all but the eastern side, with traces of a possible outer enclosure to the NW. The whole site is much overgrown.

The motte, c.12m high above the ditch to the W and 18m high above ground to the E, has an oval-shaped summit, c.34 x 15m. The bailey is roughly rectangular, c.61 x 76m, its E side showing traces of drystone walling, but elsewhere it is indicated by slight banks and scarps, and has remains of a small mound near a possible entrance gap at the NW angle. The area W of the bailey and NW of the motte, bounded to the W by a sunken track, may have been an outer enclosure.

The manor was granted by Ranulph de Meschin to Ranulph de Vaux or de Vallibus before 1122 and he, or the Scots who held the manor between 1136-57, may have founded the castle. The 'castellum de Sourebi' was first mentioned in 1186-7 concerning a £50 rent debt owed to the king by Robert de Vaux, which was apparently not repaid for when Robert died in 1195 the castle passed to the Crown. It was probably abandoned at this time as it was not mentioned in 1213 when the manor was granted to Robert de Roos, or in 1237 when the manor was granted to King Alexander II of Scotland, the grant stipulating that the land assigned to him should not include a castle. A 1300 survey of Inglewood forest describes part of the boundary as running to 'Stainwath below the castle of Soureby', the wording suggesting that the castle was in use as the usual terms for an abandoned castle etc. were 'old' or 'the site of'.

T.12(1912)pp.183-7, 22(1922)pp.114-21; Historical Castle Sowerby and Mid-Cumberland. R. Sowerby (1954)pp.26-7; EHR.74(1959) p.278; NCB p.315; OS.NY33NE/1.

HOWGILL 360401

Site of a possible ringwork destroyed sometime after 1860 when it was described as 'a circular enclosure mounded with stone and earth, about twenty-one yards [19.20m] in diameter with an opening or entrance on the south side. Large oaks have grown through the mound.' It stood on the W bank of a stream, 1½km N of Castle How.

Wh.p.520; OS.NY34SE/2.

CLIFTON   E5   NY 531270   90

A possible motte and bailey, covered by the church (12c) and churchyard situated 3½km SSE of PENRITH, and comprising a roughly circular shaped motte, c.2.44m high above the road, with an apparently crescent-shaped bailey to the NE indicated by scarps. Possibly abandoned in favour of a medieval hall and tower, the former de-molished in the early 19c. The site of the hall was excavated between 1977-9 and the few sherds of 13c pottery found

were considered to imply 'the existence, nearby, perhaps close to the church, of an earlier manor house', which in this case may have been a motte and bailey.

T.80(1980)pp.56-8, 62.

COCKERMOUTH B5 NY 12.30. 89

There are two castle sites in the Cockermouth area, although nothing remains of the site at PAPCASTLE.

COCKERMOUTH
CASTLE Parts AM 123309

The castle, originally a ringwork and bailey, occupies the end of a steep-sided ridge in the confluence of the rivers Cocker and Derwent on the N side of the town, and was originally isolated from adjoining ground to the E by a N-S cross-ditch, 7.62m wide and 5.49m deep, now filled in. The much restored and rebuilt 13c and 14c curtain walls enclose a triangular shaped area 113 x 69m, divided by a range of ruinous 14c build-ings into inner and outer wards.

The outer ward, c.57m square, was enclosed with a curtain wall in the 14c and is entered at the NE angle through a three-storey gatehouse (1), 15.24 x 9.75m, which has a projecting stair turret at the SW angle, and flanking walls projecting 5.49m from the en-trance. This ward contains the early 19c buildings, the residential block against the N wall, the stable block against the S wall, and the estate offices against the E wall, which terminate at the 14c 'Flagstaff Tower' (2), 9.45m square, projecting from the castle's SE angle. Building excavations near this tower in 1904 uncovered the foundations of a small circular tower. The W side of the ward is taken up by ruinous buildings erected between 1368-1405, including

the keep-like 'Kitchen Tower' (3), c.15.24 x 16.26m, domestic apartments (4), and an inner gatehouse (5) giving access to the inner ward, originally a ringwork and 1.83m higher than the outer ward.

The inner ward, c.27 x 34m, is en-closed by a curtain wall dating from c.1225, with the semicircular 'West Tower' (6), 7.62m in diameter dating from c.1225-1350 projecting from the apex, and the 13c 'Bell Tower' rebuilt in the late 14c or early 15c (7) 5.49 x 3.05m, projecting from the SE angle. This tower apparently guarded the original entrance of which there are some remains. The N and W side of the ward contains foundations of a 14c residential block including a hall (8), 16 x 10m.

The castle was possibly founded between 1072-1106 by Waldeve (died 1106), second son of Gospatric, Earl of Dunbar, who reputedly erected a dwelling at the mouth of the River Cocker soon after the manor had been granted to him by King Malcolm of Scotland in 1072. It may have been abandoned after the death of Alan Fitz Waldeve (died c.1150), when it passed by marriage to William Fitz Duncan (died 1152-4) son of King Duncan II of Scotland, or c.1163 when it passed by marriage to Gilbert de Pipard (died 1191) (see Papcastle below), but it was refortified between 1215-21 by William de Forz or Fortibus II, Count of Aumale, (died 1241), to whom the king had granted the manor in 1215. Because the count refused in 1221 to allow the King's soldiers to enter ROCKINGHAM castle in Northants, the king ordered that the castle of Cockermouth be destroyed 'to its very foundations', but the order was apparently ignored, for in 1241 'the castle of Cockermue' was restored to Count William de Forz III (died 1260). In 1293 it reverted to the Crown and between 1316-23 repairs are recorded to 'the little tower in the inner bailey, the little hall, the private kitchen, two bakehouses and two chambers in the same bailey, the stone wall between the two baileys, the great hall and the kitchen serving the outer bailey, the chapel, the stone walls of the prison, the new peel and the stable'. In 1323 it was granted to Anthony de Lucy (died 1343), and he or his son Thomas (died 1365), heightened the West Tower (6) and rebuilt the hall (8) with stone. It passed by marriage in 1368 to Gilbert de Umfraville, Earl of Angus (died 1381) who erected the inner gatehouse (5), domestic buildings (4) and kitchen (3), building them over the site of the inner ditch which he used as cellar space, and then dug a new ditch ahead of it. These buildings were completed by Henry de Percy, 9th Earl of Northumberland (died 1408) who acquired the castle by marriage in 1385, and he also enclosed the outer ward with a curtain wall, the work probably being in progress in 1387 when the

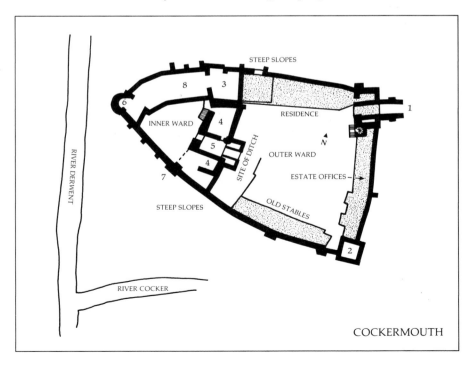

COCKERMOUTH

castle was taken and burnt by the Scots. Forfeited by the 11th earl in 1461, in 1465 it was granted to Richard Nevill, Earl of Warwick 'the Kingmaker' but was restored to the 13th Earl of Northumberland after Warwick's death at the battle of Barnet in 1471. The castle was bequeathed to the king by the 15th earl (died 1537), but was restored to the 16th earl in 1557 only to be later confiscated because of his participation in the 1569 rebellion. It remained with the Crown until c.1577 when it was restored to the 17th earl and a survey made at this time describes it as 'in great decay, as well as in the stonework as timber work thereof', and its condition had not improved by 1605 when the keeper, Sir Wilfred Lawson, reported 'The castle itself is for the most part ruinous. My wife's son dwells in the gatehouse by my direction'.

Though described in 1645 as 'neither strong nor useful', it was garrisoned for Parliament and in 1648 withstood a siege for almost a month before surrendering. In 1649 it was dismantled and the inner ditch filled in, and it remained ruinous until 1669-76 when 'the gatehouse, with two rooms adjoining, and the Courthouse [the Flagstaff Tower] at the east angle' were made habitable. In 1682 it passed by marriage to Charles, Duke of Somerset (died 1748) descending to his son and heir Duke Algernon who was created first Earl of Egremont. After his death in 1750 the castle and earldom passed to his nephew, Charles Wyndham, (died 1763) who commenced rebuilding and buttressing the curtain wall and re-roofing the outer gatehouse, but the main work of rebuilding, consolidation and additions was by the 3rd earl, Percy Wyndham (died 1837), who succeeded in 1763. It descended to General Sir Henry Wyndham (died 1861) who made some alterations, and then to his elder brother, the 1st Lord Leconfield and remains with his descendants. Occupied. OTV.

GM.67 pt.1 (1797)p.9; The Citizen No. 25 (1.7.1830) pp.755-7; T.4(1878-9)pp.109-38, 11(1911)pp. 129-58, 29(1929)pp.69-80; MMA. 1 pp.409-18; CE.2pp.304-8; CT pp.127-33, 492-6; CG.3(1969)p. 112; BE pp.107-8; CCW pp.69-73; EB pp.134-5; CL.156(1974)pp.146-9, 210-3; HBC p.475; History of Cockermouth. J. B. Bradbury (1981)pp.38-61; OS.NY13SW/6.

PAPCASTLE
or PAB(P)CASTRE, PAPSCASTLE, PIPARDS CASTLE, PIPERS CASTLE

The castle reputedly stood inside the Roman fort situated 1¼km NW of Cockermouth, but nothing of the castle or fort survives, and the site has been built over.

Gilbert de Pipard (died 1191) acquired the manor by marriage c.1163 and reputedly erected a stone fortress on the site of the fort using the stones of the fort.

T.4(1878-9)p.113; EB pp.134-5; CL.156(1974)p.146.

CORBY   E3   NY 470541   86

A 19c mansion incorporating parts of a 14c towerhouse and a 17c wing, situated above the E bank of the River Eden, 6¼km ESE of CARLISLE. The remainder of the towerhouse was demolished during the 19c rebuilding.

Gleaston Castle: the south-west tower.

In 1323 the manor was granted to Richard de Salkeld who either erected the towerhouse or rebuilt an earlier one. In 1625 it was purchased by Lord William Howard whose second son, Sir Francis (died 1660) added a wing. During the Civil War it was confiscated and not regained by the Howards until the Restoration. It was rebuilt in its present form and the towerhouse demolished between 1812-17 by Henry Howard. Occupied.

Northumbrian Castles, Churches and Antiquities. Pt.3 (1854) pp.160-68, W. S. Gibson; T.14(1914)pp.238-55; CE.2 p.308; CT pp.266-7; CL.1/1954 pp.32-5, 92-5; Arch. J. 115(1958)pp. 251-2; BE pp.110-11; CCW pp.73-6; OS.NY45SE/10.

COUPLAND ᴬᴹ (W) G6 NY 709189 91

A possible ringwork situated at the end of a broad spur between the Hilton Beck and the A.66 road, 3km SE of APPLEBY. It may have been built to guard a crossing and possibly as an outpost for APPLEBY castle. It is circular, 18.29m in diameter, and up to 2m high above outside levels. The breastwork is up to 1m high above the interior to the N and E.

In 1777 it was described as 'a round fortification internal diameter 40 paces, with walls about 10 yards thick. The stones, red in colour, were strongly cemented with lime and sand'. In 1850 it was considered to be 'the site of a round tower, or castle' and early OS maps indicate the site as a 'Roman Fortress'.

NB 1 p.610; M p.194; RC p.179; HKS p.60; OS.NY71NW/18.

CREW E1 NY 569779 86

Ruins of a probable 16c bastle house with traces of defensive earthworks, situated 229m above sea level on the slopes of Crew Fell, 3km N of BEWCASTLE.

It is rectangular, 11.28 x 8.23m over walls 1.52m thick and up to 3.05m high with entrances in the N and S walls. An inner ledge 2m above floor level was probably the support for an upper floor.

It has no known history and is called a castle only at a very late date. The earliest reference to a dwelling was in 1583 when 'Will Noble of the Crew' is mentioned.

T.10(1910)pp.102-6, 11(1911)p.57; CT p.364; OS.NY57NE/8.

CROSBY-ON-EDEN E3 NY 448596 85

A possible motte and bailey covered by the church and churchyard situated 6km ENE of CARLISLE. It comprises a roughly oval-shaped mound, c.2m high above the road, and a crescent-shaped bailey, indicated by a scarp, to the N.

CULGAITH   F5   NY 60.29.   91

Between c.1141-3 King David of Scotland issued a charter to Shrewsbury
Abbey from 'the new castle at Culchet',
possibly Culgaith situated 9½km E of
PENRITH. There are no visible remains
and the site is unknown, and Culcheth
(Lancashire) and Kelso (Borders) have
also been suggested as the possible site.

Medieval Manchester. J. Tait (1904) p.168; PNC 1 p.185; NCB p.162.

DACRE Earthworks AM   E5   NY 461265   90

A three-storey 14c towerhouse standing in the NE angle of a rectangular-
shaped enclosure, 55 x 73m, situated on
a spur of high ground S of the church,
6½km SW of PENRITH.

It is rectangular, 14.63 x 11.28m and
20m high, with projecting angle towers
of which that to the W (1) 6.40m square,
was the original entrance, blocked c.
1674 and replaced by the present entrance (2) on the eastern side. The N
and S towers (3 and 4) measure c.3.35 x
4.88m, and that to the E (5) is 7.32m
square. Foundations of parallel walls (6)
extending westwards from the W tower,
visible in the 1870s, have since disappeared. The enclosure was surrounded on all but the eastern side by a ditch,
9.14m-15m wide and c.3m deep, which
was mostly filled in c.1802, the remaining side probably being closed by a
wooden palisade or a curtain wall.

In 1307 William de Dacre received a
licence to crenellate his Manor House at
'Dunmalloght', and the 'pelem de Dunmallock' was mentioned in 1312. It is
possible that Dacre is Dunmalloght
(but see DUNMALLOGHT), and that
the original tower, probably destroyed
by the Scots in 1317-18, was replaced
by the present tower c.1350; a licence
for a chapel within the tower being
granted in 1354 to Margaret de Dacre.
For most of the 16c and 17c it was
apparently abandoned, but was altered

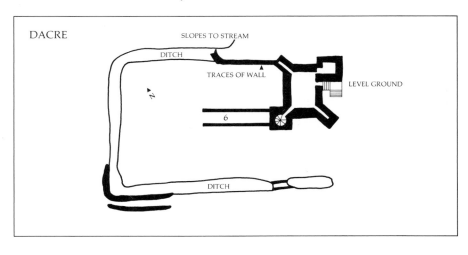

DACRE

and made habitable c.1674 by Thomas Lennard, Lord Dacre, created Earl of Sussex (died 1715), whose arms are above the entrance. After its purchase by Sir Christopher Musgrave in 1716 it was allowed to decay, and a 1739 engraving shows the outworks demolished and vegetation growing from the roof. Later in the 18c it was purchased by the Hasells of nearby Dalemain and used as a farmhouse, though as late as 1923 the upper parts were in a bad state of repair as at this time it was 'not considered safe to climb the tower'. It was restored in 1961. Occupied. OTV by written appointment only.

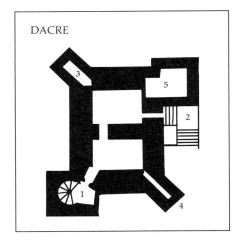

DACRE

AF pp.345-7; T.1(1866-73)pp.140-7; DAE.2 pp.213-6; OMH pp.278-86; CE.2 pp.308-10; CT pp.191, 269-72; CL.3/1929 pp.450-6; CCW pp.77-80; MA.27(1983)p.172; OS.NY42NE/1.

DALTON IN FURNESS ^{AM}   (L) C10   SD 225739   96

A three-storey rectangular towerhouse, 13.72 x 9.14m over walls 1.52-1.83m thick and 13m high, situated close to the church on the W side of the town. Built of local limestone with red sandstone dressings, it has certain architectural details which indicate a building period between 1315-50. The N end of the W wall is 2.74m thick and contains an arched passage. The original entrance was on the S side at ground floor level where a spiral staircase gave access to all floors and the roof, but this was blocked c.1704 and replaced by the present W door. The interior has been considerably altered over the years.

It was probably built by the abbots of Furness soon after the Scottish raids of 1314-16, possibly on the site of the prison/courthouse mentioned in 1257. In 1323 the abbot was ordered to 'deliver his peel near the abbey to the sheriff of Lancaster', an order that some consider referred to PIEL castle, but Dalton is more probable. At the Dissolution it passed to the Crown, and by 1545 was 'in great ruin', a survey recording 'all the floors are rotten because the roof of the said Castle is also decayed for lack of thatch. The lime of the walls is washed out, so that the said walls are partly decayed at the corners, and other places, the cost of the repairs estimated at £20 at least'. Repairs were made in 1546 using materials from Furness Abbey. Granted to the Duke of Albermarle in 1662, it passed to the dukes of Buccleuch who made many interior and exterior alterations between 1704-1856. It was used as a gaol until c.1774, and by the late 19c served as an armoury for the local volunteers. NT. OTV. GA.

T.10(1910)pp.312-30, 29(1929)pp.234-41; CE.2 pp.184-5; CT pp.191, 274-5; Arch. J. 127(1970)pp.266-7; OS.SD27SW/4.

DERWENTWATER C6 NY 28.22. 89/90

The site is unknown and whatever remained after its destruction in the 15c had completely disappeared before the early 19c. It traditionally stood near Castle Lane, on the high ground of Castlerigg, E of Keswick c.GR.28.22. Five possible sites in the vicinity viz. Bellintake, Castlerigg Hall, Causeway Head, Great Wood, and Rakefoot, were examined or excavated in 1903 with negative results.

The castle is attributed to the Derwentwaters who had settled here between 1199-1216, and whose residence at Castlerigg is mentioned c.1225. The inquisition post-mortem held in 1303 after the death of Thomas de Derwentwater mentions 'a place called Castlerigg' and also 'a capital messuage containing within the enclosure two acres.' In 1317 the manor of 'Kastelrigg' passed by marriage to the Radcliffes who allowed the building to decay, and c.1460 used the materials for a house they built on Lord's Isle, Derwentwater.

CE.2 pp.302-3; T.4(1904)pp.257-322.

DOWNHALL ^AM^ C3 NY 282525 85

Damaged earthworks of two enclosures, W and E, reputedly the site of a 12c castle attributed to Hugh de Morville (died 1202), situated at Downhall Farm, ½km SE of Aikton, 7km SSW of BURGH BY SANDS. The site was partially levelled for agricultural use in 1972.

The W enclosure comprised an island 55 x 43m, enclosed by a bank c.1m high, and surrounded by a ditch. The oval shaped E enclosure, 58 x 29m, was also enclosed by a bank, but without a ditch. About 28m to the N are remains of a wet moat, c.22m wide and c.183m long, which probably once surrounded the site.

A 'capital messuage' mentioned in 1232 was later burnt by the Scots and probably abandoned. In 1826 when excavating foundations for farmbuildings, a portion of the drawbridge was discovered, and excavations in 1972 produced large amounts of burnt timber.

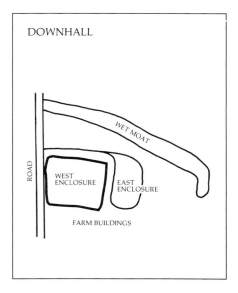

DOWNHALL

WET MOAT

ROAD

WEST ENCLOSURE

EAST ENCLOSURE

FARM BUILDINGS

T.6(1881-2)pp.194-5, 10(1910)pp.112-5, 72(1972)pp.328-9, 87(1987)pp.67-83; CT.pp.43-4; OS. NY25SE/5.

DRUMBURGH C3 NY 268598 85

This three-storey tower of c.1500, incorporating some 13c work, stands in the village, 5km W of BURGH BY SANDS, and was probably built to guard fords crossing the Solway Firth. Remains of a ditch to the N (at GR. 264599), may be part of the 13c defences, but other remains visible in the early 20c to the S and W, have since disappeared.

The tower is rectangular, 22.86 x 8.23m over walls c.1.22m thick, with a pitched roof and an entrance in the N front reached by a steep flight of steps. The arms of Thomas, Lord Dacre (died 1525), are above the entrance which was moved to this position when the original, immediately below at ground floor level, was blocked. The ground floor incorporates part of a possible early 13c stone hall, with windows and an elaborate door, all blocked.

The early remains are probably those of the 'dwelling house at Drumburgh' for which Robert le Brun received a licence to crenellate in 1307. Early in the 15c it passed by marriage to Jacob Harington, who allowed it to decay, and by c.1485, when it passed to the Dacres, it was ruinous. It was probably rebuilt by Thomas, Lord Dacre, and c.1538 Leland noted that 'the Lord Dakers father built upon old ruins a pretty pile for the defence of the country - The stones of the Pict [Hadrians] Wall were pulled down to build Drumburgh for the wall is very near it'. By c.1580 it needed 'urgent repairs' and in 1593 it was described as 'neither castle nor tower but a house of strength occupied by a bailiff'. In 1646 Mr. Cuthbert Orfeur, who had held it 'for many years from the Earl of Arundel' requested that it be restored to his possession having been 'violently ousted by John Hodgson, agent to Lord Dacre'. Ruinous by 1678 it was purchased by John Aglionby from Henry, Duke of Norfolk and was acquired by exchange in 1696 by Sir John Lowther who restored it, altering the windows and blocking the original doorway. During the 20c it again fell into decay, but by the 1970s was being restored. Occupied.

T.11(1911)pp.241-2, 20(1920)pp.220-2, 29(1929)pp.205-10; CE.2 p.311; CT pp.188, 202-3; CCW pp.84-5; MA.23(1979)p.270; OS.NY25NE/1.

DUNMALLOGHT E6 NY 46.24. 90

In 1307 William de Dacre (died 1318) received a licence to crenellate his house at 'Dunmalloght', and Ranulph de Dacre's 'pelem de Dunmallock' is mentioned in 1312. The inquisition post mortem held after the death of Humphrey, Lord Dacre in 1485, makes no mention of a castle or a towerhouse, but does mention 'the wood at Dunmallock'. The castle or fortified house is assumed to have stood at the N end of Ullswater, but the actual location is unknown, though Dunmallet, an Iron Age hill-fort at GR. 468246; Trostremont, a possible homestead moat at GR.467236, and DACRE have been suggested as the possible site.

T.1(1866-73)pp.157-61, 3(1878)p.248, 11(1911)pp.233-5; 12(1912)pp.99-101, 37(1937)p.55, 38 (1938)pp.42-3; CT pp.47-8, 204; RC p.39; PNW.2 p.215; Arch. J. 132(1975)p.36; OS.NY42SE/2.

A motte and bailey, with substantial masonry remains, formed from the summit of a steeply scarped hill, now a park, on the W side of the town. It comprises a circular motte at the higher N end of the hill with a rectangular-shaped walled inner bailey to the S, and an inner ditch c.3.05m deep and 8m wide, to the W and S. Except at the S end the castle is surrounded at a lower level by a platform, up to 10m wide, which probably served as an outer bailey, and has a bank to the NW, up to 1m high, and an outer ditch, c.7.62m wide and 3.05m deep, to the E.

The motte is 5m high above the bailey and 12m high above the platform. Its summit, c.18m in diameter, formerly carried a circular keep built c.1200. A considerable portion of the keep remained in 1816, and parts survived until c.1860, but except for a large piece of fallen masonry on the motte's northern side, it has disappeared. The bailey, 37 x 31m, is enclosed by remains of a curtain wall, 1.52m thick, built c.1170 and heightened c.1350, which on the W outer side has a large section of herring-bone masonry (1). The E curtain contains remains of a postern gate (2) with foundations of buildings adjacent to both sides (3); those to the S are of a c.17c court house. To the N, separating the bailey from the motte are the walls of the hall, etc. and the inner gatehouse (4), while projecting from the SW angle is the ruinous main gatehouse (5), 11 x 9m, built c.1130-40 but mostly refaced in the 14c; this also has some herring-bone masonry and originally controlled a drawbridge, now replaced by a cause-way. A circular tower formerly projecting from the S curtain (6) has disappeared.

The outer bailey was reputedly enclosed by a palisade with a fortified gate on or near the side of the modern gate (7), and excavations in 1922 outside the N limits of the castle revealed a NW-SW L-shaped section of 'an old and massive wall' (8), each section c.6.10m long and up to 1.22m thick and estimated to have been 3.35m-4.27m high. It was later discovered that the NW wall had been c.23m long and had terminated at a circular tower or bastion (9), suggested to be the site of the castle's 'Town Gate'. There was another circular tower at the S end of the E side of the bailey (10) which guarded an entrance.

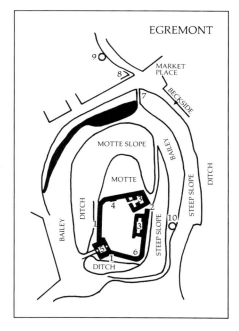

The castle was probably founded early in the 12c by William le Meschin (died c.1134), brother of Ranulf, who was granted most of Cumberland in 1093

by William II, and passed by marriage to Robert de Romilli of Skipton. In 1138 the castle withstood a Scottish attack, and c.1140 it passed by marriage to William fitz Duncan (died c.1151), nephew of King David I of Scotland, then to Reginald de Lucy (died c.1199), and c.1215 to Lambert de Multon (died 1246) to whom the hall block is attributed. In 1315 and in 1322 it was attacked by the Scots, probably suffering some damage, and in 1335 it passed by marriage to Robert Fitz Walter of Essex. In 1371 the castle was mortgaged to raise £1000 ransom demanded for the release of Walter Fitz Walter, then held prisoner in Gascony. It remained with the Fitz Walters until c.1444 when it passed by marriage to John Radcliffe of Norfolk, (died 1461), whose son John became the sixth Lord Fitz Walter. After Lord John's death in 1496 he was succeeded by his son Robert, created Earl of Sussex in 1529, and in that year he sold the castle to Henry, fifteenth earl of Northumberland (died 1537). Earl Henry, in 1535, bequeathed the castle to the king, and after his (the earl's) death it was abandoned and allowed to decay. It reverted to Thomas, the sixteenth earl (executed 1572), and when surveyed for the next earl in 1578, it was described as 'now all most ruinated and decayed save that some part of the old stone work and walls thereof are yet standing and one chamber therein... in like ruin and decay. About the castle is a pleasant dry ditch, and outside the ditch has been a base court now called the Castlegarth'; the whole covered about 2 acres. In 1682 it passed by marriage to Charles Seymour, eleventh Duke of Somerset (died 1748), and on the death of the twelfth duke in 1750 it passed by marriage to the Wyndhams who were earls of Egremont (title now extinct), later created lords Leconfield and lords Egremont, who still own the castle. OTV.

T.6(1881-2)pp.150D-162D, 23(1923)pp.133-7; CE.2 pp.312-4; GD pp.4-20; CT pp.23, 134-7; Cumberland News 5.3.1932; EHR.74 (1959)p.267; EB p.115; NCB pp.181, 183; CCW pp.85-7; CFH pp.225, 272, 376-7; ASLD pp.78-81; OS.NY01SW/1.

GLEASTON ᴬᴹ   (L) C10   SD 261714   96/97
or MUCHLAND

This ruinous castle stands on ground sloping N to S, adjoining Castle Farm, in a valley bottom, situated 1km NNE of the village, 7¼km SSW of Ulverston. It was quadrangular, c.79 x 55 x 44m, with large angle towers and an entrance at the NW angle. It was built of roughly squared undressed local limestone, with red sandstone quoins, doors and window surrounds. There are no traces of interior buildings or outer defensive works, but the southern towers survive basically intact. The N curtain had probably been built only above foundation level before its destruction in the late 14c., and the bend in the W curtain, indicated by remains of a buttress, is probably due to a change of plan during its construction. The main residence was the NW tower, 28 x 13m, built c.1340 on ground 9m higher than that to the S, which contained a large lower chamber with a stair to the upper floors, but only some walls up to c.9m high survive. The NE tower, built only to curtain wall height, measured 17.68 x 9.14m but only one wall survives. The SE tower, 9.45 x 13.11 x c.11m high,

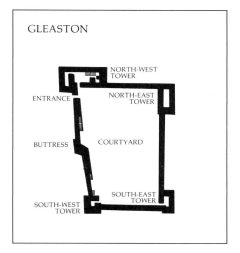

GLEASTON

was the only one with direct access to the rampart walk. It has remains of a turret at the NW angle as also has the SW tower which measures 10 x 9.45m, and is 13m high.

In c.1107 the manor was granted to Michael le Fleming 'and from him the manor took the name of Michael's land or Muchland' which also included ALDINGHAM. It passed by marriage to William de Cancefield in 1269 then c.1300 to his nephew John de Harrington to whom the castle is attributed. After the death of Sir William Harrington in 1458 the castle was abandoned and passed by marriage to William, Lord Bonville, killed at the battle of Wakefield in 1460, who reputedly ordered its dismantlement. It passed by marriage to Thomas Grey, created Earl of Huntingdon in 1471 and Marquess of Dorset in 1475 (died 1501) and c.1538 Leland noted 'a ruin and walls of a castle called Gleston Castle'. In 1542 the third marquess, Henry Grey, leased the manor and castle to his bailiff Walter Curwen who later purchased them outright, holding them until early in Queen Elizabeth I's reign when they were acquired by Thomas Preston. Possibly at this time or later one of the southern towers was made habitable as c.1639 a 'Richard Gaitskell of Gleaston Castle' is recorded, and it apparently remained inhabited until after 1693. It passed by descent to the Cavendish family and between 1914-18 the castle was sold by the Cavendishes of Holker Hall to the owners of the adjoining 'Castle Farm'.

AF pp.81-2, 211, 310, 386-8; T.13(1893-4)pp.37-49, 6(1906)pp.184-90, 24(1924)pp.260-5, 361-4; CCA.1 pp.110-2; The Antiquary 5 (1882)pp.102-4; FCN pp.114-9; CE.2 pp.187-8; CT pp.142-4; OS.SD27SE/27.

GREYSTOKE E5 NY 435309 90

A mainly 19c mansion incorporating a towerhouse and walling of 14c date, standing on an eminence W of the village, 8km W of PENRITH. It is naturally protected to the W and S, and there may have been a ditch to the N and E. The towerhouse, c.10.67m square, is incorporated into the NW angle, but only part of the W wall is visible. This and the E wall are 1.52m thick, while the N and S walls are 2.44m thick. The site has been occupied since c.1130, but the earliest visible remains are those of the manor house of 'Craystock' for which William de Greystock received a licence to crenellate in 1353. The manor house, reputedly quadrangular with angle towers, passed first to the Grymethorpes, and then, c.1506, to the Dacres from whom it was confiscated in 1569.

Samuel and Nathaniel Bucks' 1739 view of Highhead Castle.

It was later acquired by Philip Howard, Earl of Arundel (died 1595) and remains with his descendants who became heirs to the dukedom of Norfolk. During the Civil War it was held for the king until its capture in 1648, when the greater part of it was destroyed by fire. It apparently remained derelict until c.1675 when it was rebuilt by Henry Howard. The 16th duke (died 1786) and the 17th duke (died 1815) made many alterations including heightening the towerhouse and demolishing the SW tower. Occupied.

T.13(1913)pp.205-6, 24(1924)pp.156-8; CE.2 pp.314-5; CT pp.190, 205; History of Greystoke, V. S. Stafford-Howard, MS, Carlisle Record Office; CCW pp.89-91; OS.NY43SW/7.

HARTLEY Parts AM   (W) G7   NY 786082   91

Fragmentary remains situated on a spur of high ground 1km SE of Kirkby Stephen. The castle was demolished between 1704-35 and the present house, also called 'Hartley Castle', was built on the site of the outer court, incorporating some fragments. Remains near the house comprise rubble walls, a cellar with a segmental barrel-vault, and a medieval mask corbel built into the garden wall. There are no associated earthworks, though traces of an oval-shaped settlement at GR.787084 may indicate the predecessor to the 14c castle.

The manor, possibly with a manor house, was confiscated c.1315 from Roger de Clifford and granted to Andrew de Harcla. Forfeited in 1323, it was granted to Ralph de Nevill of Raby. It was later purchased by Thomas de Musgrave (died 1385) who received a licence to crenellate his manor house at 'Harcla' in 1353, because it was 'situated near the Scottish March and has frequently in the past been burnt and destroyed by our enemies the Scots'. Two wings were added c.1600 by Richard de Musgrave (died 1615) 'transforming it into a mansion' and in 1671 it was described as 'a stately house and seat, which hath received many additions by its present owner'. It was abandoned c.1677 and a 1692 sketch shows that it comprised a thick, high curtain wall enclosing a square outer court, with an inner court enclosed by three and four-storey buildings. By 1773 there was 'Scarcely a wreck left of the castle', materials having been removed to repair Eden Hall.

OMH pp.159-63; CE.2 pp.286-7; CT pp.189, 207-8; RC p.101; OS.NY70NE/12.

HAYES AM   A6   NY 003227   89
or AYKERIST, AYKHURST, DYKHURST, HAY (it is first called HAYES in 1600)

It is situated on low-lying ground adjacent to Hayes Castle Farm, on the S side of Distington, 5km NE of Whitehaven, and comprises a mound, c.34m square and 2.44m-3.05m high above the surrounding moat, which is c.1.52m deep and 6m wide. The masonry castle was probably quadrangular c.28m N-S x 22m E-W, but only part of the N curtain remains, c.0.91m thick, 5.49m high and 12.80m long.

In 1322 Robert de Leyburn, keeper of EGREMONT Castle, received a licence to crenellate 'his dwelling house at Dykhurst', and the 'forcelet of Aykerist' was mentioned in 1374. It passed to, and was abandoned by, Christopher de Moresby (died 1392) and after his death was described as 'a greatly ruined castle'.

By 1794 it comprised 'a gloomy old tower on an artificial mount surrounded with an outward or curtain wall, supported by many heavy buttresses', but by 1816 all that survived were foundations 'and a portion of the N wall'. The NW angle of the curtain wall was demolished in 1933 and the materials used in the adjacent farm buildings.

T.16(1916)pp.29-39, 25(1925)p.351; CE.2 p.315; CT pp.188, 279-80; OS.NY02SW/1.

HAYTON   B4   NY 110417   85
(Aspatria)

A two- and three-storey house, dating mainly from c.1665, but incorporating walls 0.99-2.13m thick, of an earlier building, situated at the E end of the village 2¼km W of ASPATRIA. It is rectangular, c.15.24m E-W x 27.43m N-S, the well preserved N wall incorporating remains of a rectangular tower, c.9.14 x 8.23m.

In c.1420 when the manor passed from the Tilliols to the Colvilles, a dwelling was rebuilt by William Colville (died 1479), which comprised a central block with rectangular towers attached to the

N and S ends. It passed to the Musgraves in 1479 and in May 1568 Mary, Queen of Scots spent one night here. Heavy damage received during a Parliamentary siege in 1648 necessitated an almost complete rebuild, most of which was carried out c.1665 by Sir Richard Musgrave who altered the floor levels, inserted new windows, and moved the main entrance from the E to the W side. By 1794 it was 'much neglected', and by at least 1860 used as a farmhouse. It has since been restored and modernised. Occupied.

T.13(1913)pp.234-43; CT pp.373-4; CCW pp.92-3; OS.NY14SW/8.

HAYTON ᴬᴹ   E3   NY 507578   86
(Castle Hill)

A damaged and overgrown ringwork formed from the end of a narrow scarped ridge, 15m-24m high, situated in the village NW of the church. It was isolated from adjoining ground to the E by a ditch, traces of which remain, and if there was a bailey it lay beyond this

ditch. A breastwork, up to 1m high, encloses an area c.19m in diameter.

It was possibly founded by the de Vaux family who were granted the manor by Henry II.

T.6(1881-2)pp.466-7; CT p.40; CG.3(1969)p.112; OS.NY55NW/9.

HIGHHEAD   D4   NY 403433   85
called HEHED 1370, HEIGHHEVED 1375, HYGHETT, HIGHENED and HIGHED 1549, HIGHYATE 1576, HEGATCASTLE 1692, HIGHGATE 1750

The burnt out shell of this mainly 18c mansion stands on a steep sided rocky promontory surrounded on all but the N side by the River Ive, and is situated W of Ivegill, 13km S of CARLISLE. It comprises the 18c mansion, 27.43 x 15.85m, incorporating at the W end a mid-16c building with mullioned windows, and projecting diagonally from the SW angle a rectangular building (1) 7.32 x 5.49m, possibly on the site of a 14c tower.

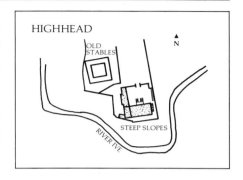

The tower of 'Heyheved', first mentioned in 1323 concerning its garrison, was granted in 1327 to William L'Engleys, Chief Forester of Inglewood (died c.1369); but because by 1331 it was in decay and its foundations weak, William built anew, presumably on the same site, and in 1342 received a licence to crenellate his manor house at 'Heyheved', first referred to as a castle in 1357. Between 1369-75 it passed by marriage to the Restwold family who sold it in 1542 to John Richmond, and he and his descendants lived here until

c.1739 when it passed by marriage to Henry Richmond Brougham (died 1749). A view of the castle drawn in 1739 shows it in a somewhat neglected condition with vegetation growing from the walls, and a crenellated curtain wall enclosing a rectangular shaped area with a two-storey gatehouse and portcullis projecting from the N wall, and the main domestic building forming the W side. Between 1744-8 with the exception of the W side of the castle, the whole was demolished and replaced by the present mansion, which was un-

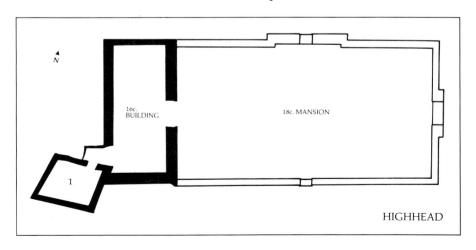

finished internally in 1749 when it passed by marriage to two co-heirs each of whom owned one half. Because of legal difficulties regarding the joint possession, neither party could occupy the castle, though the 16c portion was apparently occupied by a farmer, and to solve the problem one of the co-heirs commenced pulling down his half sometime between 1774-8 in order to sell the materials. Luckily before the demolition had proceeded too far the castle was purchased by the first Lord Brougham (died 1868). In 1902 it was purchased and partly restored by the Hill family, remaining occupied until December 1956 when, with the exception of the western side, it was gutted by fire. Restoration work commenced in 1988 had ceased by early 1989 and it was put up for sale in the October.

T.2(1874-5)pp.105-8, 11(1911)pp.379-84; CE.2 pp.316-7; CT pp.189, 209-10; Cal. of Inquisitions, Miscellaneous (Chancery) 2 (1307-49)pp.305-6, 1973; CCW pp.94-5; Cumberland News 20.1.1984, 3.2.1985, 23.1.1987, 20.10.89; OS.NY44SW/3.

HOLME CULTRAM   C4   NY 177509   85

Earthworks beside the B.5307 road N of the abbey may be remains of a motte and its ditch, or remains of a rampart and ditch thrown up around the abbey precincts by the monks in the late 12c.

The 'capital messuage' possibly the castle of Alan fitz Waldeve (died 1139) was mentioned in the 12c, and regulations for coastal patrols, issued in 1552, records one between the 'Brownrigge Kiln and the Castlehill at Holme Cultram'.

T.1(1866-73)p.266; CT p.40; Register of Holme Cultram. F. Grainger and W. Collingwood (1929)pp.121, 174; OS.NY15SE/6.

HOWGILL   (W) G5   NY 669292   91

Built of rough ashlar, mostly rendered over, it is basically an 18c rebuild of a late 14c tower, and stands in an elevated position 1km E of Milburn church, 9½km NNW of APPLEBY. It comprises a three-storey central block (1), 10.67m square, with attached wings (2), 15.55 x 9.45m.

Soon after acquiring the manor from his kinswoman, Margaret de Ros, Roger de Lancaster (died 1291) may have erected a dwelling which was replaced by a tower before 1354 when John de Lancaster dated his will from 'Howgill Castle'. In c.1438 it passed by marriage to the Crackenthorpes who added a hall

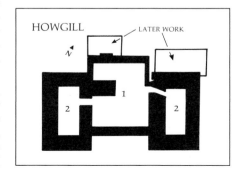

block to the N side, but this was demolished between 1509-47 when the N and S wings were added by the Sandfords who had acquired it by marriage. In 1651 it was garrisoned for the king by Sir Richard Sandford (murdered in London in 1675), who had 'purchased twenty muskets' for the purpose, and it may have suffered some damage at this time. It passed by marriage in 1723 to the Honywoods who c.1733 remodelled the castle which included heightening the central block and removing parapets from both wings. About 1780 they sold it to the Tufton family. Before 1851 it was used as a farmhouse, but was later allowed to decay, and by 1967 it was described as being in 'a semi-derelict condition'. It has since been restored. Occupied.

OMH pp.142-7; CE.2 pp.287-8; T.9(1909)pp.198-201; CT pp.281-3; RNW pp.161-2; RC p.174; CCW pp.95-6; OS.NY62NE/1.

IRTHINGTON   E3   NY 49.61.   86

There are two motte and bailey sites here, one adjacent to the church and the other 1km NE at the eastern end of the village adjacent to the former mill. This latter site was possibly abandoned in favour of the former.

MOTTE AND BAILEY ᴬᴹ 499614

An overgrown, truncated motte situated immediately E of the church, with no trace of the surrounding ditch or of the bailey which lay to the SE, both of which had completely disappeared before the mid-19c. The motte was c.9.14m high with base and summit diameters of c.54 and 23m respectively, and was surrounded by a ditch c.9m wide, but by 1858 it had 'been lowered many years since, to form a garden on the summit'. The farm adjacent to the motte's W side reputedly stands on the site of a masonry building, 'which measured about 96 feet by 75 feet, with a tower at the S angle, and perhaps at the others also. The middle of the castle was about 50 yards from the mound and about 10 yards clear of the ditch which surrounded that elevation'.

In 1158 Hubert de Vaux (died 1165) was granted the barony of Gilsland, of which Irthington was part, and the castle may have been founded by him or his son Robert (died 1195). Irthington is said to have been the 'chief messuage' of the barony, but there was a possible motte at Gilsland (Northumberland). In c.1240 the barony passed by marriage to the de Multons, and c.1317 to the Dacres who abandoned the castle in favour of NAWORTH. The castle at Naworth is said to have been 'enlarged and improved out of the ruins of the castles of Irthington and Kirkoswald'.

T.4(1878-9)pp.484-5, 12(1912)pp.181-3; SRW pp.67-9; CE.2 p.317; CT p.23; OS.NY46SE/4.

IRTHINGTON MILL 508623

Only the roughly oval shaped motte survives c.3m high with base and summit diameters of 46 x 18m and 18 x 8m respectively. Earthworks immediately

N of the motte are thought to be connected with the former mill.

T.23(1923)p.209; OS.NY56SW/15.

| KENDAL | (W) E8 | SD 52.92. | 97 |

There are two sites in Kendal: CASTLE HOWE to the W of the town and KENDAL CASTLE to the E.

CASTLE HOWE 512923 ᴬᴹ

A motte and bailey occupying the E end of a ridge on the W side of the town, and originally comprising a circular motte at the end of the ridge with a roughly kidney-shaped bailey across the ridge to the E. The motte remains but the bailey has been mostly built over.

The motte, c.15m high above the bailey, has base and summit diameters of c.46 and 18m respectively. It was isolated from the bailey by a semicircular ditch, material from which was used to form the motte. The summit was enclosed by a breastwork which has mostly disappeared.

The bailey, c.60m E-W x 80m N-S, was defended by a steep slope to the E and by a ditch to the N and S which joined with that of the motte.

Ivo de Taillebois (died c.1094) was granted the barony soon after 1087 and may have founded the castle, or it may have been founded by Ketel who was granted the barony by Henry I. It was possibly abandoned by Ketel's son, Gilbert, or by Gilbert's son, William (died c.1170) who assumed the name 'de Lancaster' early in the reign of Henry II.

T.8(1908)pp.97-102; CT pp.30-1; RC p.122; EB pp.56-7; ASLD pp.82-5; OS.SD59SW/5.

KENDAL CASTLE ᴬᴹ 522925
or KIRKBY-KENDAL

A ringwork with masonry remains situated on the summit of Castle Hill, 91m above sea level, E of the town. Remains of a curtain wall, 1.52-2m thick and up to 9m high, enclose an area 76m in diameter, with remains of a circular NW tower (1) 7m in diameter, a keep (2) 10.97 x 9.14m to the S, a hall-block (3) 24.38 x 9.14m to the NE, traces of a possible barbican (4) 34 x 29m outside the entrance, and a semi-circular bastion (5) on the W side. The castle is surrounded by a ditch 3m deep and 26m wide, and an outer bank c.3m high.

Possibly founded by either Gilbert, or his son William (see Castle Howe above), it passed by marriage c.1184 to Gilbert Fitz Reinfred (died 1220) to whom the masonry castle is generally attributed. It was confiscated in 1215 but was restored by Henry III to Gilbert's son William, who had assumed the name of 'de Lancaster', and after his death in 1246 it passed to Peter de Brus. In c.1272 it passed by marriage to the de Roos family, and from them, in 1383, to the Parrs the most famous of whom, Katherine, widow of Henry VIII, is often said to have been born here, but she was born in Northamptonshire. In 1553 the castle was confiscated from William Parr, Marquess of Northampton, but was restored to him in 1559, and after his death in 1571 it passed by exchange to the crown. It was ruinous at this time and a survey made in 1572 records 'The out walls embattled 40 foot square - within the same no building left, saving only on the north side is situate the front of the gatehouse. The hall with an ascent of the stairs to the same, with a buttery and pantry at the end thereof, one great chamber and 2 or 3 lesser chambers, and rooms of ease, adjoining the same, all being in decay both in glass and slates and in all other repairs needful. Under the hall are two or three small rows of cellars. In the south side is situated a dove-cot. The walls are circular, guarded by three towers and a keep, with a large square area in the centre, being all in a state of

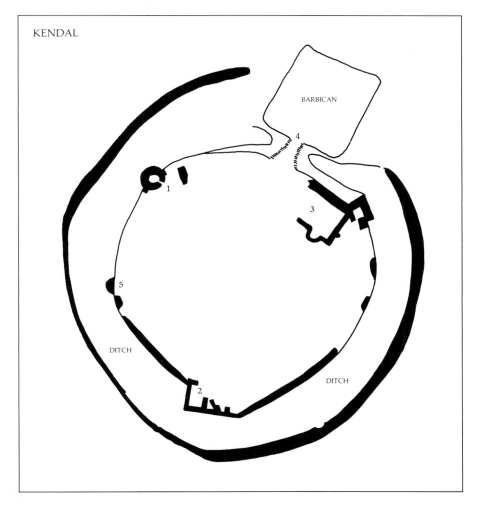

KENDAL

BARBICAN

DITCH

DITCH

dilapidation. In its doors and window jambs, and in a few quoins we find the red sandstone, but the main work is built with unhewn blue rock from the hills.' By 1578 'most part of the roofs are fallen down, the timber and slate pitifully broken, the gutters of lead, iron in windows and doors pilfered and stolen away - there will be little left to sell within short time'.

Elizabeth I granted it to Ambrose Dudley, Earl of Warwick (died 1590), and it was later acquired by the Fanes, earls of Westmorland who sold it c.1667 to Sir Charles Anderton. It was resold in 1728 and a print made in 1739 shows most of the curtain wall intact and the keep and other towers ruinous but standing almost to their full original height. In 1813 the then owner 'strengthened foundations' and 'took many other wise precautions to stay the fall', and before its acquisition by Kendal Corporation in 1896, the owner Lord Bentinck 'spent a large sum' on consolidation work. The site was excavated between 1967-72. OTV.

T.1(1866-73)pp.71-80, 2(1874-5)pp.186-96, 9(1888)pp.178-85, 8(1908)pp.84-102, 51(1951)pp. 185-6; CE.2 pp.288-90; CT pp.145-9; RC pp.122-4; EB pp.56-7, 77-78; MA.12(1968)p.179, 13(1969)pp.260-1, 16(1972)p.183; CCW pp.105-8; ASLD pp.82-5; OS.SD59SW/2.

KIRKBY LONSDALE ^{AM} (W) F9   NY 611789   97
(Cockpit Hill)

A motte situated on a bluff above the steep W bank of the River Lune, N of the church. The E side has been damaged, and the summit dished, possibly to adapt it for use as a cockpit. There is no trace of a bailey. It is 5.79m high above remains of the surrounding ditch, and has base and summit diameters of c.40 and 24.38m respectively.

T.5(1905)p.278; CT p.35; RC p.136; OS.SD67SW/10.

KIRKCAMBECK   E2   NY 533689   86

The church and churchyard occupy a possible truncated motte or a ringwork, a roughly triangular area c.43m each way and c.2m high above the roads which surround it. There may have been a bailey to the E, and the short ridge extending S, now occupied by a farmhouse, may also have been a bailey or possibly the site of the castle.

Between 1154-89 Alfred Cammock had a 'capital messuage' here but the site is unknown, though there must have been a substantial building here in 1307 when the king and queen and their retinue stayed here from March 1st to the 4th before continuing to LINSTOCK. In c.1923 a 12c motte was recorded at Howdale Farm, situated 1km W of the church, but there are no visible remains, and the occupant of the farm in 1980 had no knowledge of a mound or its possible site.

T.23(1923) p.209; Magna Britannia. 4 p.xv (1816) D. and S. Lysons

KIRKOSWALD F4 NY 55.40. 90

The main castle site is situated SE of the village; there is also a moated site on low-lying ground SW of the church.

CASTLE ^{AM} 559409

The castle is situated on rising ground SE of the village and comprises a much overgrown enclosure, 116 x 92m, surrounded by a moat up to c.2m deep and 9-12m wide.

On the N side are remains of a restored stair turret and a postern (1), on the S side are remains of the curtain, c.4.57m high, and the basements of two towers, while elsewhere there are grass covered foundations and blocks of fallen masonry. The original entrance is on the W side (2), the mound (3) to the N of it may be a truncated motte, but the inset at the SE angle (4) is probably due to the topography.

The castle was quadrangular, c.46m square over walls 2.44m thick, with a recess, 9.14 x 17m in the SE angle, and the main entrance in the W side. Rectangular towers (5) 10.67 x 9.14m, projected from the southern angles, and others, 7.62m square (6) and 6.71m square (7), flanked the entrance. The stair turret (1) 4.42m square, which projected diagonally from the N curtain, was 20.73m high, but has been reduced to its present height of 19.81m by the removal of its battlements. It originally gave access to three floors, and to the roof of an adjoining building.

A wooden tower, reputedly built at Kirkoswald in the 12c by Ranulph Engaine, may have stood on the castle site or on the moated site (see below) and the history of the castle until the early 14c may refer to the latter. By 1158 it had passed by marriage to Simon de Morville (died 1167) whose son, Hugh (died 1202) received a licence

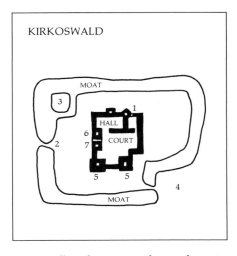

KIRKOSWALD

MOAT

HALL COURT

MOAT

to crenellate his manor house here in 1201. It passed by marriage first to Richard de Lucy of EGREMONT, and c.1213 to the de Multons. In 1298 Isabel, widow of Thomas de Multon III (died 1294), married John de Castre, a Nottinghamshire landowner (died c. 1324), and in 1310 Thomas de Multon IV granted him the castle for life, probably because of the marriage, but also because together with Thomas III he had made additions to the castle. It was reputedly burnt by the Scots in 1314, and in 1317 passed by marriage to Ranulph, Lord Dacre (died 1339) who abducted the heiress, Margaret de Multon from Warwick Castle. After the death of Humphrey, Lord Dacre in 1485 a 'castle newly built' was mentioned, indicating some extensive building or rebuilding, which his son Thomas (died 1525) 'did finish and moat about with great charge'. Forfeited because of the Dacres' involvement in the 1569 rebellion, it later passed by marriage to Lord William Howard, but from 1569 until c.1601, when Lord William regained the castle, etc. by paying Queen Elizabeth £10,000 'to redeem his possessions', it was allowed to decay, and between 1604-24 was gradually stripped of its materials, some of them going to NAWORTH. By 1688 it was 'a bare shell or heap of stones' and after its purchase by Sir Christopher Musgrave c.1715 it gradually reduced to the few ruins remaining today.

T.2(1874-5)pp.1-10, 12(1912)pp.164-80; OMH pp.262-71; CE.2 pp.318-20; CT pp.150-3; NCB p.218; CCW pp.112-3; OS.NY54SE/2.

MOATED SITE 555409

A very large moated site situated on low lying ground immediately SW of the church. To the NE it is overlooked by a high hill, the summit of which has the appearance of having been artificially scarped, but this may have been done when the church tower was erected there in the 19c. The proximity of the hill and the fact that this may be the site burnt by the Scots in 1314, may have induced the Dacres to build a new castle on a new site described above. The site, best viewed from the summit of the hill, comprises a double ditched rectangular enclosure, c.250 x 175m, the ditches c.4m wide and 15m apart. In the centre of the enclosure is a low rectangular mound, c.20 x 50m, surrounded by a ditch, 5-8m wide.

OS.NY54SE/13.

LAMMERSIDE AM   (W) G7   NY 773048   91

A ruinous 14c tower built of rough rubble from which most of the facing stones have been removed, situated in an isolated position, above the W bank of the River Eden, 3km S of Kirkby Stephen. It can be seen from the B 6259 road. Buildings, formerly attached to the N and S sides are indicated by grass covered mounds, and to the E are traces of an enclosure.

The tower is rectangular, 13.72 x 11.28m, over walls c.1.52m thick and now c.4.57m high, with a N-S corridor suggesting that this was the buttery-wing, with the main domestic buildings on either side. The ground floor comprised five vaulted chambers, and the second floor, three chambers and a garderobe. The N and S foundations indicate rectangular buildings, c.16.76 x 7.32m and 10.67 x 11.28m respectively.

It was probably built by the de Warcops to guard one of the main routes to the south, and was possibly occupied by the Whartons prior to the erection of Wharton Hall c.1415. By 1536, when occupied by a 'Mr. Warcop', it was probably in decay, and is thought to have been abandoned later in the century. In c.1801 when called 'Lammerside Hall' it was described as 'a very ancient square tower'.

T.4(1904)pp.85-91; CE.2 p.291; CT.291; RC p.240; OS.NY70SE/1.

The moated site at Kirkoswald, seen from the hill behind the church.

LAZONBY   E4   NY 549398   90

A possible motte and bailey situated in the village 1½km SW of KIRKOSWALD and comprising a massive mound with what appears to be a bailey to the NE, now occupied by the church (the original was built c.1157) and churchyard.

There is no documentary evidence or tradition of a castle here, and it has been suggested that the mound is spoil from the adjacent Carlisle-Settle railway built c.1875, but this is unlikely. The 1845 Tithe Map has a plan of the village showing a large mound W of the church, with a house on the summit called, suggestively, 'Seathill', which was demolished and apparently part of the mound removed, when the station was built. The lower E slope of the mound has always been part of the churchyard, and the remainder of the eastern half was purchased as an extension for the churchyard in 1898.

LIDDEL STRENGTH ᴬᴹ   D2   NY 402742   85
or LIDDEL MOTE

A motte and bailey, possibly originally a ringwork and bailey situated high above the S bank of the River Liddel, which here forms the border between England and Scotland, 18km N of CARLISLE. It was never a masonry castle (i.e. it was without masonry curtain walls).

The motte (1), possibly a later addition, and damaged by landslip on the E side, is 25m high above the ditch to the E and S, and has base and summit diameters of c.27m and 11m respectively. The inner bailey (2) 61 x 55m, possibly originally a ringwork, is defended to the N and E by a slight bank and the steeply falling ground, but to the W and S there is a semi-circular bank c.11m high, and a ditch 8m deep, together 18m across. This bailey contains traces of a rectangular building (3) c.10 x 8m, possibly the tower erected c.1348 by Sir Thomas Wake. The outer bailey, 55 x 69m, has similar northern defences to those of the inner, but with a lesser bank and ditch to the W and S. The oval-shaped mound (4) at the eastern end of the ditch is probably the site of a guard tower.

The early history of the castle is often confused with that of Liddel Castle, situated 19km NE in Roxburghshire, Scotland, founded c.1130 by Ranulph de Soulis. Most of north Cumberland was granted to Ranulph de Meschin in 1092 and before 1121 he had granted the manor of Liddel to Turgis Brundis (died c.1130) who may have founded the castle. Turgis was succeeded by his son William, called both Brundis and de Rosedale, who was an adherent of the Scottish king and consequently was allowed to retain the lands and castle when Cumberland was ceded to the Scots in 1136. In 1157 when Cumberland reverted to the English Crown both manor and castle were granted to Nicholas de Stuteville (died 1206) who not only had a claim to them by marriage, but was also loyal to King Henry. (References in various histories to Ranulph de Soulis, nephew of Ranulph le Meschin succeeding to the manor and castle in 1170, are probably referring to Liddel castle in Scotland where he was reputedly murdered in 1207). Nicholas was holding the castle in 1174 when it

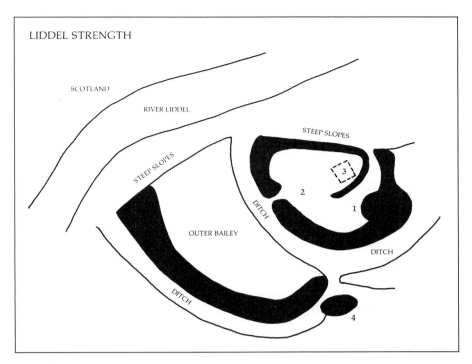

LIDDEL STRENGTH

SCOTLAND

RIVER LIDDEL

STEEP SLOPES

STEEP SLOPES

DITCH

OUTER BAILEY

DITCH

DITCH

was taken by William the Lion, but it was later recovered and remained with the de Stutevilles until 1217 when the king ordered the sheriff 'to take possession of the castle and vill'. It was restored to the de Stutevilles c.1220 and in c.1233 it passed by marriage to the Wakes.

After the death of Baldwin Wake in 1282 the inquisition post mortem refers to 'Lydel, the site of a castle containing a wooden hall, with two solars, cellars and a chapel, also a kitchen, a byre, a grange and a wooden granary which threatens ruin but might now be repaired'. In 1300, when held during a minority by Simon de Lindsay, 'warden of Lydel and Ermitage Soules', he was ordered to 'repair the Mote and the fosses around it, strengthening and redressing the same and the pele and the palisades, and making lodges within

the mote if necessary for the safety of the men-at-arms' of the garrison'. In 1346 two hundred men led by Sir Walter Selby held out for four days before the castle was taken and destroyed by David II of Scotland, who executed Sir Walter and both of his sons, but it was later retaken and repaired and probably at this time the masonry tower was erected. After the death of Thomas Wake in 1349 it passed by marriage to John of Woodstock, created Earl of Kent in 1351, who gave the castle to the king, and in 1357 it was granted to John of Gaunt, Earl of Richmond, reverting to the Crown after his death in 1399. It was probably abandoned at this time as it was not mentioned at all throughout the 15c, and the fact that Leland, who visited the site between 1536-43, noted only that 'mote ledale was a moated place' making no mention of any buildings, does suggest that it was no longer in use. It was probably replaced by 'Highmoat', a large moated site situated ¼km SW, and this, not the castle, was probably the 'Mote of Liddale' burnt in 1528 by the Scots during a Border affray. Before 1553 the manor had been acquired by the Grahams who reputedly erected a hall and a chapel in the castle, but again it is probable that 'Highmoat' is meant, as is the statement that the castle was abandoned between 1603-25. The 'square tower of excellent' masonry noted at Liddel Strength in 1794 had disappeared before the late 19c.

T.9(1888) pp.404-8, 10(1910)pp.91-101, 13(1913)pp.33-54, 26(1926)pp.390-7, 29(1929)pp.49-56; CE.2 pp.320-1; CT pp.24-8; EB p.129; BNC.37(1965-7)pp.50-3; BCP pp.132-4; CG.5(1972)p.108; NCB p.225; CCW pp.121-2; OS.NY47SW/1.

LINSTOCK   D3   NY 429586   85

A 14c red-sandstone, two-storey tower-house, 9.75x10.67m over walls 1.37m thick, incorporating some earlier work, situated 4km W of CARLISLE. It was rebuilt and modernised c.1768 by James Nicolson who replaced the flat roof with a gable, inserted new windows, and replaced the original entrance which was at first floor level. A modern house incorporating 15c work is attached to the S side, and there are traces of the surrounding ditch to the W and N.

The bishops of Carlisle acquired the manor c.1219-23 and by c.1230 had erected a dwelling, large enough by 1307 to accommodate the king and his retinue for six days. Abandoned as a residence c.1450 it was used as a prison and as a place of refuge, and by at least the mid 17c was used as a farmhouse. About 1842 the interior comprised 'four apartments. That on the ground floor is vaulted, and is lighted by one narrow window at the western end, and has no communication with the upper chambers. The apartment on the first floor, which like the vaulted chamber beneath, occupies the whole area of the building, is converted into a modern parlour, and from it, by a flight of stone stairs formed in the thickness of the wall, there is an ascent to the second floor, which is divided and forms two commodious apartments'. It was sold by the Church Commissioners in 1863.

OMH pp.342-3; CE.2 p.321; T.12(1912)pp.187-94; CT pp.298-9; CCW pp.122-4; OS.NY45NW/9.

LOWTHER   (W) E6   NY 51.24.   90

The 'castellum de Lauudre' mentioned in 1174 and again in 1287-8, may be the enclosure called CASTLESTEADS, or it may be covered by the shell of LOWTHER CASTLE, a 19c mansion. These two sites are situated ½km S and ¾km SSE of the church respectively, 6½km S of PENRITH.

PNW.2 p.184

CASTLESTEADS 519241   (W)

A rectangular shaped univallate enclosure measuring 28 x 22m, with a large oval-shaped mound forming the SE angle, situated in a plantation on the edge of ground falling steeply to the River Lowther. It has the appearance of a small motte and bailey, but is suggested to be the site of a towerhouse or other later medieval building. Traces of a ditch visible earlier in the century have since disappeared. The surrounding bank is up to 1.22m and 4.57m high above the interior and exterior levels respectively, and has an entrance gap in the E side. The mound is 2.44m-3.05m high and has a summit diameter of c.6.40 x 9.14m.

RC p.160; OS.NY52SW/3.

LOWTHER CASTLE 522239   (W)

The shell of this early 19c mansion occupies the site of Lowther Hall, built between 1272-1307, which reputedly replaced a motte and bailey (for 19c mansion see Appendix).

RNW p.329.

MARYPORT ᴬᴹ   A5   NY 033362   89
(Mote/Castle Hill)

A damaged ringwork (1), its W side destroyed by subsidence, situated in a commanding position at the end of a high steep-sided spur on the S side of the town in a loop of the River Ellen. If there was a bailey it lay to the N, but this side has been built over. The ringwork is c.6m high above the surrounding ditch, which is c.3m deep and 6m-9m wide, and has base and summit diameters of 52 and 26 x 18m respectively. The breastwork at the N end widens to form a mound (2) possibly the site of a guard tower, and to the S is an isolated mound (3), c.3m high with a summit c.7.40m in diameter. A causeway (4) leading into the ringwork's NE angle may be original, as may be the path rising from the bottom of the spur to the causeway.

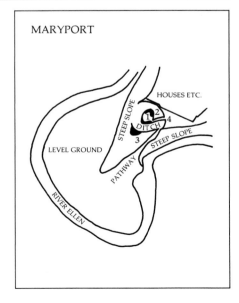

MARYPORT

T.14(1914)p.488, 23(1923)pp.146-7, 26(1926)p.414; CT p.41; CG.3(1969)p.112; OS.NY03NW/8.

MILLOM ^{Parts AM}   B9   SD 171813   96

Substantial remains of a 14c fortified manor house situated on rising ground 1km N of the town and occupying the summit of a possible motte, isolated from ground to the W and S by a semi-circular shaped ditch, c.3.05m deep and 9.14m wide, all that survives of the original surrounding ditch. To the S are scarps of a possible kidney-shaped bailey, covered by the late-Norman church and part of the churchyard.

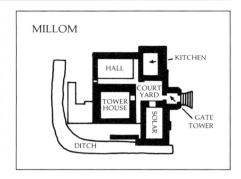

The ruinous gate tower, 6 x 8m, is approached by a flight of steps which replaced a drawbridge, and the kitchen, 7 x 8m, probably rebuilt in the late 14c or early 15c, incorporates some earlier work. Of the hall, 14 x 10m, only the N and W walls survive, 1.83m and 1.37m thick respectively. The towerhouse, 15.24m square and 13.41m high is now the farmhouse, its original E entrance converted into a window. Remains of a solar, 13 x 6.71m, fill the SE angle.

The manor was granted to Godard de Boyville in 1134 and he may have founded the motte and bailey, possibly to replace an earlier motte or motte and bailey which reputedly guarded the Millom Ford crossing the Duddon Estuary. In c.1240 the manor passed by marriage to the de Hudlestons, John de Hudleston receiving a licence to crenellate his Manor House at 'Millum' in 1335, and he added the towerhouse, possibly on the site of an earlier tower, the gatehouse and the hall. There were some alterations and additions c.1450, and c.1460 it was damaged by the Lancastrians though not enough to cause its abandonment. In 1622 Ferdinand de Hudleston received a licence to crenellate, probably using it to make good anything then in disrepair, but in 1644 it was taken and slighted by the Parliamentarians, and probably at this time the remainder of the motte ditch was filled in. Some repairs were made c.1671 but it fell into decay and by 1739, except for the towerhouse, was the ruin we see today. In c.1748 it passed by marriage to Sir Hedworth Williamson who sold it c.1774 to Sir James Lowther. The towerhouse is occupied and forms part of the farmhouse. Occupied.

T.1(1866-73)pp.275-7, 24(1924)pp.180-234, 83(1983)pp.85-99; CE.2 pp.321-2; CT pp.189, 211-2; Lake District History. W. G. Collingwood (1928) p.75; CCW pp.133-4; ASLD pp.86-91; OS.SD18SE/11.

MUNCASTER   B8   SD 103965   96

This red granite and sandstone castle stands at the end of a spur high above the Esk Estuary, possibly on an earlier fortified site, 1½km E of Ravenglass and was originally isolated from ad-joining ground by 'artificial earthworks', probably a bank and ditch. The castle is rectangular, c.58 x 18.29m, with a tower and a towerhouse, both c.12.19m square projecting W from the two western angles. Extensively remodelled in 1783 and rebuilt in 1862, it incorporates a 14c towerhouse at the SW angle and other medieval walling in the N side, all that remains of a larger castle built c.1325. The four-storey towerhouse with walls c.2.44m thick at base, has a spiral staircase to the roof in the NE angle, and another in the SW angle from a tunnel-vaulted basement to the first floor.

By 1185 the manor was held by Benedict de Pennington (died between 1199-1216), the main branch of the family moving here c.1242 from PENNINGTON, and later changing their name to 'de Mulcaster'. The castle remains in the possession of their descendants. Occupied. OTV. GA.

Wh. pp.489-92; CE.2 pp.322-3; GD pp.201-5; CT pp.308-9; BE p.165; CCW pp.137-41; OS.SD19NW/6.

NAWORTH   F2   NY 559627   86

It stands near the end of a roughly triangular shaped steep sided promontory between two streams, 3¼km NE of BRAMPTON, and was isolated from adjoining ground to the E by two N-S cross-ditches, c.18m wide and c.31m apart. Part of the inner ditch remains, used as a sunken garden.

The castle is an irregular rectangle, its shape governed by the promontory: the curtain wall, 2.44m thick and 7.93m high to the rampart walk, measures on each side, W.35m, N.55m, S.54m and E.69m. The main gate (1) gives entrance into a courtyard, 31 x 40m, enclosed on all but the S side by buildings, with the 'Howard Tower' (2) forming the NE angle, the five storey 'Dacre Tower' (3) at the SE angle, and the 'Morpeth Tower' (4) outside the NW angle. The 'Howard Tower', built c.1520, is unusual in that it consists only of upper storeys carried upon a series of arches spanning the angle between the curtain walls. The 'Dacre Tower' is a towerhouse, 8.84m square, over walls 2.90m thick at base reducing to 2.29m above, and is 18.29m high. It was built c.1335 on the site of an earlier tower, parts of which are incorporated and it has a postern gate beside it.

The two towers (5 and 6) outside the E curtain, one a gatehouse called the 'Warden's Tower' (5), are all that remain of a small outer court, measuring 76m N-S. There are modern buildings (7) attached to the W curtain.

Ranulph de Dacre (died 1339) acquired the manor c.1317 by marriage (with Margaret de Multon, whom he abducted from Warwick Castle) together with a ruinous tower reputedly destroyed by the Scots at this time. In 1335 he received a licence to crenellate his Manor House at 'Naward' which then consisted of the Dacre Tower and an enclosure, both strong enough by 1346 to withstand a Scottish attack. The castle was remodelled into its present form c.1520 by Thomas, Lord Dacre (died 1525) who incorporated the Dacre Tower into the SE angle and added the fifth storey. After the death of George, fifth Baron Dacre in 1569 who at the age of seven 'was by great mischance slain at

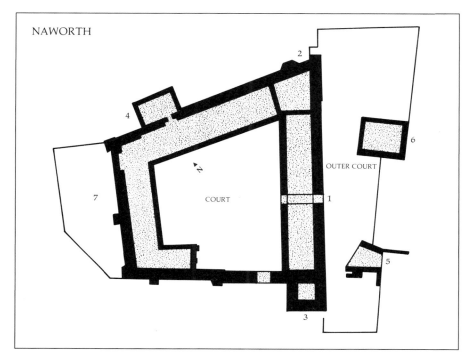

NAWORTH

COURT

OUTER COURT

Thetford [Norfolk] in the house of Sir
Richard Palmerstone, by means of a
vaulting horse of wood, standing within
the same house; upon which horse, as
he meant to have vaulted and the pins
at the feet not being made sure, the
horse fell upon him, and bruised the
brain out of his head' it passed to three
co-heiresses, all of whom married into
the Howard family. Before they could
take possession it was seized by their
uncle, Leonard Dacre, from whom it
was confiscated because of his involvement in the 1569 rebellion and it fell
slowly into decay.

In 1589 it was described as 'a fair
castle - of good strength and built four
square with a gatehouse to the same.
One of the squares thereof has never
been finished further than the walls
thereof, of two or three stories high. It
is all covered with lead - and it is now in

very great decay in all parts and the
outhouses and other houses and offices
are utterly decayed'. In 1601 Lord
William Howard (Belted Will) (died
1640) gained possession of the castle
and various estates on payment to the
Crown of £10,000, and in the next
twenty years spent most of his income
on restoring the castle, adding the
Howard Tower, and using internal fittings purchased from the owners of
KIRKOSWALD castle. The restoration
of the castle was completed c.1624 and
was then occupied by himself and his
family said to number 52 persons, taking
into account their wives, husbands and
children. During the Civil War it was
garrisoned for Parliament by Sir Charles
Howard and consequently was not
damaged, and because in 1660 Sir
Charles strongly advocated the return
of the monarchy, he not only retained

the castle, but was also created Earl of Carlisle in 1661. In May 1844 the E wing was gutted by fire, the newspapers reporting 'The flames were first discovered about four o'clock in the afternoon, and, although the fire engines from Carlisle arrived [by train] in less than two hours, the roof of the hall had then fallen in, and the flames were fast progressing towards the large tower.

The fine old feudal residence was almost a heap of ruins, but, fortunately, the tower containing the apartments occupied by Lord William Howard [Belted Will] was very little injured'. The castle was restored and the 'Morpeth Tower' added between 1845-6 by George, Earl of Carlisle, and also at this time the defences of the outer court were removed. Occupied. OTV. GA.

Northumbrian Castles, Churches and Antiquities, W. S. Gibson, pt.3 (1854) pp.1-42; Surtees Soc. 68 (1877) pp.lxiv-lxxiii; T.4(1878-9)pp.486-95; CE.2 pp.323-7; CT pp.188, 213-8, 503; BNC.34 (1956-8)pp.221-31; BCP pp.144-7; CCW pp.141-6; CL (2/1987)pp.74-9, 88-91; Fifteen Famous English Homes. R. Churchill (1954)pp.39-47; OS.NY56SE/1.

ORMSIDE, GREAT   (W) G6   NY 701177   91

A possible motte with a bailey or village enclosure to the E, situated on the S bank of the River Eden, overlooking a ford, 2¾km SE of APPLEBY. The 14c tower incorporated into Ormside Hall stands immediately SE.

It comprises an oval-shaped mound 3.66m-6.10m high above surrounding levels, its summit c.36 x 52m, covered by the church, which dates from the

11c, and the churchyard. In a field to the E are traces of a large circular enclosure surrounded to the E and S by remains of a moat. The mound is 'partly natural and partly artificial' and has been suggested as a probable early burial mound. Its size is similar to the motte or ringwork at APPLEBY castle which is 52m in diameter.

T.4(1878-9)pp.182-3 notes, 15(1897-8)p.377, 23(1923)pp.278-9; RC pp.185-6; RNW p.189.

PENDRAGON AM   (W) H7   NY 782026   91

The name reputedly derives from Uther Pendragon, father of King Arthur, who according to tradition died here. It is probably the MALVESTANG castle mentioned in 1228, and also the castle of MALLERSTANG mentioned later in the 13c.

It consists of a ruinous square tower built of local rubble occupying the end of a ridge which has been isolated from adjoining ground to the N by a semi-

circular shaped ditch, with traces of a possible bailey across the minor road to the NE. It is situated beside the B.6259 road 5½km S of Kirkby Stephen and is in the process of consolidation. The tower, originally of three storeys, but now only up to second storey level, is 19.51m square over walls 3.66m and 3.05m thick on the N and S, and E and W sides respectively, with a garderobe turret projecting diagonally from the

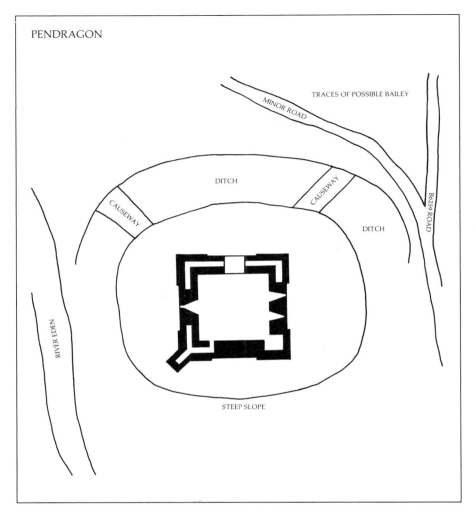

PENDRAGON

SW angle. The interior is filled with fallen rubble concealing various openings and has an entrance in the N side. The ditch, c.3.05m deep and 9.14m wide, is crossed by two causeways to the NW and NE.

Hugh de Morville (died 1202) reputedly erected a fortress here c.1180 but he probably built it before, or soon after, the forfeiture in 1173 of his castles at APPLEBY and BROUGH. Pendragon was apparently forfeited at a later date, as in 1203 together with the latter castles it was restored to Hugh's nephew, Robert de Vipont (died 1264), and c.1269 passed by marriage to Robert de Leyburne. After de Leyburne's death in 1283 it is mentioned as 'the castle of Mallerstang', and in 1308 his widow granted it to her nephew Robert de Clifford who received a licence to crenellate in 1309 and reputedly enlarged and strengthened it. After his death at the Battle of Bannockburn in 1314 it passed to his son Roger, a minor, and the custody of the castle was given to Guy Beauchamp, Earl of Warwick (died 1315). When Roger came of age in 1321 he joined the Earl of Lancaster's rebellion and was taken at the Battle of Boroughbridge in 1322 and executed, and the castle was confiscated and granted to Andrew de Harcla, Earl of Carlisle. After de Harcla's execution in 1323 the castle reverted to the Cliffords and was burnt by the Scots in 1341. It was rebuilt between 1360-70 by Robert de Clifford and remained inhabited until 1541 when it was accidently destroyed by fire, being described in 1610 as 'a great heap of stones'.

In 1643 it passed to Anne Clifford, Countess of Pembroke who rebuilt it between June 1660 and October 1661, and later wrote 'I did cause a wall of lime and stone to be built round about that piece of ground which I had taken in about the castle, ninety roods in compass, with two gates to let in horses and coaches and within the said wall I caused to be built a stable, coach-house, brew house, bakehouse, washhouse, and a little chamber over the gate that is arched.' The countess was a frequent visitor until her death in 1676, but by c.1685 it had been dismantled by the Earl of Thanet to whom the vast Clifford estates had passed by marriage. A 1739 engraving shows the parapet walls and the windows built into the guard turrets intact, but by 1773 the upper parts had fallen, and before the late 19c all of the dressed stone had been removed. Lord Hothfield placed it in the care of EH predecessors in 1928, and in 1963 it was purchased by Mr. R. Frankland with the intention of clearing the interior of rubbish and consolidating the remains.

T.2(1902)pp.408-9; OMH pp.33-5; CE.2 pp.291-2; PSN.3(1908)pp.258-61; CT pp.66-7, 120-1, 454; RNW pp.56, 102, 121-2, 282; RC pp.163-4; Mallerstang, A Westmorland Dale. M. Thompson (1965) pp.13-18; NCB pp.274-5; CCW pp.154-5; HLC p.2; The Independent 17th Oct. 1989; OS.NY70SE/2.

PENNINGTON ^{AM} (L) C10 SD 258777 96
(Castle Hill)

A ringwork formed from the end of a steep sided promontory, situated adjacent to Castle Farm ¾km NW of the church, 3km W of Ulverston. A public footpath runs through it. An open area below the SW side, closed by a bank to the SW and the Pennington Beck to the NW, may have been a bailey.

The ringwork is roughly oval-shaped, c.48 x 40m in diameter, and is isolated from adjoining ground to the N and E by a semi-circular shaped bank, c.0.91m-1.83m high, and a ditch. There is an entrance gap in the eastern side.

Traditionally this was a castle of the de Pennington family abandoned c.1242 in favour of MUNCASTER. The 'capital messuage' of William de Pennington mentioned in 1318 is the manor house site at Beckside situated ¼km SSW of the church at GR.260773. (See also the Appendix).

T.6(1906)p.316; FCN p.224; VCH(L)2 p.555; CT p.37; CG.3(1969)pp.98,117; OS.SD27SE/13.

An extensive red-sandstone ruin mainly of the late 14c-early 15c, situated on high ground adjoining the railway station on the W side of the town.

It comprises a ruinous curtain wall, 1.52m thick, in places almost to its full original height, enclosing an area c.40m square containing around the courtyard (1), which measures 21.34 x 19.81m, foundations and walls of various buildings and towers including a garderobe turret (2) projecting from the western wall. As originally built it comprised a walled enclosure, probably with timber built lean-to buildings around a central courtyard, exterior central and angle buttresses, except at the E angle (3) which contained a chamber for smoking meat, and the Strickland Tower (4), 10.06 x 8.84m, guarding the entrance. The buildings were rebuilt with masonry early in the 15c when the castle was remodelled, and the Red Tower (5), 8.53 x 9.14m, added to guard a new entrance (6). An outer gatehouse was added to the Red Tower c.1471 when more buildings were erected, and there were minor additions and alterations between 1485-1603. The Strickland Tower collapsed between 1739-78 and only low restored walls, 2.29m thick, survive.

The manor, granted to John de Dreux, Duke of Brittany, in 1378 was forfeited in 1382, but during his brief ownership he granted a perpetual lease of land in Penrith to William de Strickland together with the right 'to construct a fortalice within the town in which he [the duke] would have the right to stay unhindered when in those parts'. In 1397 William received a licence to crenellate for his 'chamber', and two years later received another licence 'to make a

mantlet of stone and lime and join it to the same chamber and crenellate the same'. It was later granted to Ralph Nevill, Earl of Westmorland, who remodelled it early in the 15c, and remained with his descendants until 1471 when it was granted to Richard, Duke of Gloucester, later Richard III, who made minor alterations and additions. Although described c.1539 as a 'strong castell of the King's', it was in decay, and in 1547 large amounts of masonry were removed. A 1565 survey records the buildings decayed and the outer gateway 'mostly collapsed', and another survey in 1572 records that though some of the buildings were in good repair except for their roofs, the outer gatehouse (7) was in 'utter ruin', three stables were ready to collapse, the chapel, the great chamber, the great hall, the two kitchens, and all other offices 'were not repairable' and 'many cartloads' of stone had been removed. Some repairs were made but it was

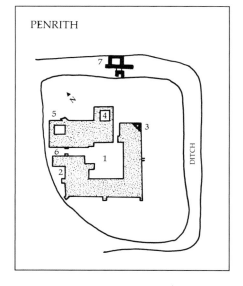

PENRITH

generally allowed to decay, and the only notable event in its later life was during the Civil War when it was occupied for a month in 1648 by General Lambert who used it as his headquarters. In 1694 it was granted by the king to his Dutch favourite, Hans William Bentinck, created Earl of Portland in 1689 (died 1709), and was sold in 1787 by a descendant, the 3rd Duke of Portland, to his brother-in-law, William, Duke of Devonshire (died 1811). His descendants sold it c.1840-5 to the Lancaster and Carlisle Railway (later incorporated into the London and North Western Railway), and it was acquired in 1913 by the Penrith Urban Council. It was presented to the EH predecessors in 1914 who excavated and consolidated the ruins c.1928. OTV.

OMH pp.244-52; CE.2 pp.327-8; T.18(1918)pp.174-88, 30(1930)pp.12-26; CT pp.189-90, 219-23; HKW.3 pt.1 pp.226n, 403; CCW pp.155-8; ASLD pp.58-63; OS.NY52NW/1.

PIEL ^{AM}　　　　(L) C11　　　　SD 232636　96
or PELE/PILE of FOTHERAY/FOULDREY

Though much eroded away by the sea there are still substantial remains of this castle which stands at the S end of Piel Island, situated at the mouth of the entrance to Barrow-in-Furness harbour.

It comprises inner and outer wards measuring 36 x 49m and 106m square respectively, both enclosed by remains of curtain walls, 2.44m thick and up to c.4.57m high, and ditches c.2.44m deep and 7.62m wide. The outer curtain has remains of three two-storey angle towers (1), c.4.57m square, that to the NE (1A) probably one of two which flanked the entrance, and adjacent to it are remains of a chapel (2). The curtain of the inner ward has remains of three angle towers (3), and a two-storey gatetower (4), 6.10m square, which originally controlled a drawbridge. This ward contains the ruinous three-storey keep, 24.38 x 22.86m, and now c.14m high, having had its battlements and six octagonal turrets removed. A garderobe turret (5) 4 x 10m, formerly at the SE angle together with the E wall have been destroyed by the sea. The gatehouse (6) into the keep had portcullises and doors at both ends, and a stairway

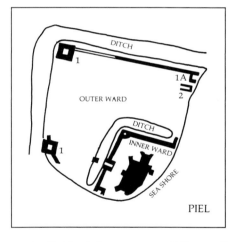

PIEL

on the E side giving access to all floors of the keep and to a room over the gate passage. On the beach adjacent to the castle's southern side are many huge blocks of fallen masonry, some weighing many tons.

King Stephen granted all his lands in Furness and Walney to the Abbot of Furness on condition that the abbot would 'make, sustain, repair, and guard a fort here'. There are no visible remains of this period and no documentary

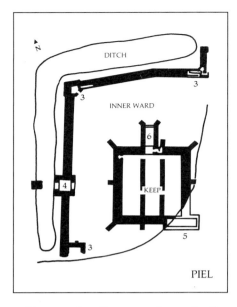

evidence exists for an early castle, the first definite mention of a fortification being in September 1327, when Abbot John Cockerham received a licence to crenellate his 'dwelling house at Fotheray'. In c.1403 the 'pele de Fotheray' was dismantled by Abbot John de Bolton because its upkeep was beyond his means, but this was considered to break the agreement made

with Stephen and it was confiscated and not restored to the abbots until 1411. Repairs made in 1429 were sufficient only to make it partially habitable, and by 1537 the 'Castelle and Pele' was 'sore decayed, and specially the covering and timber-work thereof, insomuch that £300 will scarcely repair it sufficiently'. It was abandoned and in 1588 was described as 'an old decayed Castle, parcel of the dutchy of Lancaster'. The Royalists did consider refortifying the castle during the Civil War, but it was too far gone, and at the Restoration it was granted to George Monck, Duke of Albermarle. After the death of the second duke in 1688 it passed to the Duke of Buccleuch whose descendants still own it. By 1727 the sea had destroyed all of the southern outer defences and part of the inner curtain, and by 1781 all the eastern defences including part of the E wall of the keep were washed away, the remainder of the latter being destroyed by 1860. Consolidation of the castle, begun c.1860, continues. EH. OTV.

A ferry service runs daily, subject to local weather conditions, from 1200 hrs to 1800 hrs Easter - October, other times by request. Tel. No. 0229 22520.

AF pp.368-74; T.3(1876-7)pp.232-40, 10(1910)pp.271-87, 87(1987)pp.101-16; CCA.1 pp.129-32; CE.2 pp.185-7; CT pp.188, 224-6; HKW.3 pt.1 p.179n; MA.29(1985)p.168; OS.SD26SW/3.

ROCKCLIFFE   D3   NY 354619   85
or ROCLIFFE, ROKELE

It stood on the N bank of the River Eden 7km NW of CARLISLE but there are no visible remains and the site is occupied by Old Hall and part of a minor road. When this part of the road was realigned c.1901 a pavement of cobbles, reputedly part of the castle courtyard, and a N-S red-sandstone wall, 1.37m thick and

17.37m long was uncovered. This wall and the parallel garden wall of the hall, c.28m to the E, which is built on old foundations, are considered to indicate the castle area, and in the early 20c a field W of the hall showed 'indications of further traces of the castle'.

In 1539 Leland noted 'a pretty Pile or Castle of the lord Dakers', which was seized and garrisoned by Leonard Dacre during the 1569 rebellion, and subsequently forfeited. In 1580 it was 'nothing or lytle decayed', and c.1583 'Rokele Castel the farthest strength of the west borders' was ordered to be 'kept as in William lord Dacres time'. Acquired by Anne, Countess of Arundel c.1601, in 1603 it was used as a prison for the Grahams, and c.1607 was described as 'a little castel built not long since by the Lord Dacres for their own private defence'. In 1682 it was purchased from Henry, Duke of Norfolk by the Revd. Charles Usher, and whatever remained was demolished c.1730 to make way for the hall.

T.2(1902)pp.412-3, 10(1910)pp.108-12, 39(1939)pp.156-8; CT. pp.391-3; OS.NY36SE/2.

ROSE   D4   NY 371461   85

The residence of the bishops of Carlisle, it stands near the W bank of the River Caldew, 10km SSW of CARLISLE, and occupies the bailey of the original motte and bailey castle, possibly founded by Hervey Fitz Maurice, from whom the manor was confiscated in 1186. It is an L-shaped building of two wings dating mainly from the 19c but incorporating some earlier work. The 19c 'Percy Tower', standing at the S end of the W wing, is built over the site of 'Pottingers Tower' (1). The motte, which stood on the 'Hop-garth', adjacent to the W side of 'Kites Tower' (2), was demolished between 1769-87, and the material used to fill up part of the surrounding ditch. The bailey lay to the E and covered c.0.20 hectares; traces of its ditch remain.

The manor was granted to the bishops of Carlisle in 1230 and before 1255 they had erected a masonry building, part used as a prison by 1287. It was occupied by the King and Queen for most of September 1300, and burnt by the Scots in 1314 and again in 1322, but had been reoccupied before 1332, and in 1336 Bishop John Kirkby (1332-53) received a licence to crenellate his manor house called 'La Roos'. He probably added the 'Constables Tower' (3) and a curtain wall, but in 1337, possibly when the work was in progress, it was again attacked and burnt by the Scots. A second licence to crenellate was granted in 1355 for 'La Rose' to Bishop Gilbert Welton (1353-62), and he added a hall block and possibly 'Pottingers Tower' (1). Bishop William Strickland (1400-19) rebuilt the 'Lords Tower' which had been built c.1297 by Bishop John de Halton (1292-1324), and is now called 'Stricklands Tower' (4). It is a two-storey building, 8.84m square over walls 2.29m thick, with an entrance on the S side at first floor level, and a 19c semi-circular stair-turret. During the Civil War when garrisoned by the Royalists the castle was described as comprising 'several buildings in form of a Quadrangle with five Towers and other Turrets, incompass'd also with a mantle Wall which had several little Turrets, or Room in it'. Captured and slighted by Parliament in 1648 'forty-one of its forty-nine rooms were destroyed', and in this condition was sold in 1650 to William Heveningham who occupied the W wing and made the principle entrance through 'Kites Tower' 9.75 x

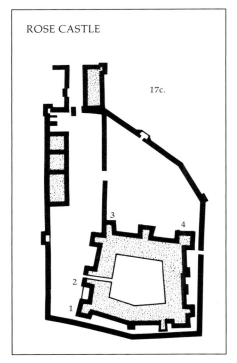

ROSE CASTLE

17c.

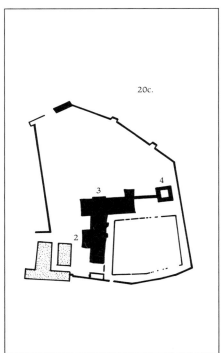

20c.

6.71m (built 1522-4 by Bishop Kite).

In 1660 the castle was restored to the bishops, and a rebuilding programme was commenced by Bishop Stern which included the demolition of the S and E wings. Stern received c.£4,000 to carry out the work, but all he did before his elevation to York, complained his successor, Bishop Rainbow, was 'to make its condition worse', continuing 'All the rooms of the ancient dwelling house on the N, E and S sides, and part of the W beginning at Constables Tower and taking in Pottingers Tower, which contained forty-one rooms, are either totally demolished or ruinated or made useless - that the walls of seventeen or eighteen rooms, which when Archbp.

Stern came were strong and firm to the roof or near it and had no such defects, but such as might have been repaired at a small charge, were taken down or broken while his Grace was Bp. of Carlisle.' The rebuilding was completed, and between 1762-9 many improvements were made by Bishop Lyttleton who described it as 'a very commodious and agreeable mansion'. Between 1829-31 it was completely renovated by Bishop Percy when the 'incongruous mixture of architectural styles introduced by successive bishops when making necessary repairs gave way to a uniform plan'. Part of the W wing was altered c.mid-1950s to provide better accommodation. Occupied.

T.2(1874-5)pp.152-65, 56(1956)pp.132-41; CE.2 pp.329-30; English Episcopal Palaces (Province of York) ed. R. S. Rait (1911) pp.235-306; Rose Castle. J. Wilson (1912); CT pp.189-90, 227-34; BE pp.181-2; CCW pp.160-3; TAMS.27(1983)pp.61-67; OS.NY34NE/3.

SCALEBY Parts AM   E3   NY 449625   85

Situated on low-lying ground 8km NE of CARLISLE, it has no natural defences and was surrounded by a double moat of which the outer, 12m wide and enclosing an area 125m in diameter, is complete. There are traces of the inner moat (1).

The castle is roughly rectangular, c.28 x 26m and comprises a ruinous 14c towerhouse (2) at the NE angle, a polygonal forebuilding (3) attached to its western side, the entrance (4), a domestic block to the S (5) and the hall (6) to the E. They enclose a courtyard c.12m square. Much of the lower masonry of the castle dates from the early 14c, but the remainder, except the

S wing which was added c.1597, is much-restored 15c work.

The towerhouse, 12.50 x 8.53m, over walls 2.13-2.44 thick, was built in 1307 and rebuilt between 1349-1367. Its three upper floors have collapsed as have the S and part of the W walls, but in the SW angle are remains of a circular stairway which gave access to all floors. The original entrance in the W wall was covered by the later fore-building, and the present entrance from the hall is modern. The forebuilding (3), 5.79m in diameter, which was added after the towerhouse was rebuilt, is open at the top and is thought never to

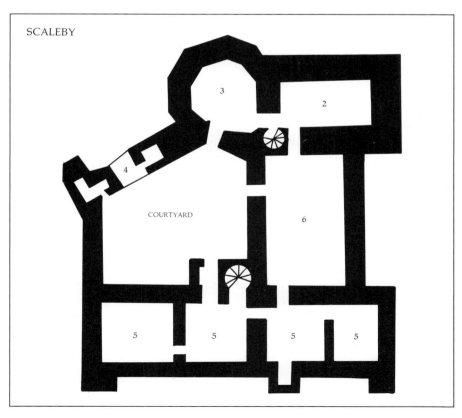

SCALEBY

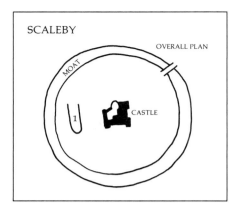

SCALEBY

OVERALL PLAN

MOAT

CASTLE

1

have been roofed, so that the interior could be overlooked from the ramparts of the tower in case of attack. The N curtain, 10.67m long and c.2.44m thick, contains the entrance, 1.83m wide, originally closed by a door and a portcullis with guard chambers on both sides, and a portcullis chamber above. The hall, 6.40 x 11.28m, the upper part of which was raised or entirely rebuilt c.1550, has a tunnel-vaulted ground floor, rare in England but common in Scotland, which being stone was probably an insurance against fire. The three-storey S block, c.27 x 7.62m, built c.1597-1600 by Sir Edward Musgrave, replaced the original kitchens and the S curtain with its three projecting turrets or bastions. This block was altered in the 18c and rebuilt c.1835-40.

Richard de Tilliol, possibly a relative of Humphrey de Tilliol who held HASTINGS castle (Sussex) in 1066, acquired the manor between 1100-35, but lost it in 1136 when Cumberland was ceded to the Scots. When Cumberland reverted to the Crown in 1157 the king restored the manor to Richard's grandson, Peter (died 1183), but no dwelling of any sort was mentioned here until 1246 when 'a capital messuage with houses' was recorded. The earliest

work that survives can probably be attributed to Robert de Tilliol (died 1321) who received a licence to crenellate in 1307, his tower being mentioned in 1317-18 when it was damaged, or possibly destroyed, by the Scots. It was first called 'castle' in 1367 and at this time probably consisted of the rebuilt tower enclosed by a palisade and a moat, the remainder added later by Peter de Tilliol (died 1435). After Peter's death it passed to two co-heiresses, Isabella Colvill and Margaret Moresby, who c.1450 remodelled the interior. In 1580, when called a 'house or castle', it was 'partly decayed, and repairing whereof is estimated to three score pounds, besides new casting of the moat'. In 1583 'Skalby castell' was described as 'a strong house and fair - not kept by any soldiers, nor skantly any dweller in it' and c.1596 it was purchased by Sir Edward Musgrave. Held by the Royalists in 1644 it was besieged for 'many months' but not taken until a second siege in February 1645, when it it thought to have been badly damaged and burnt. It was re-garrisoned by the Royalists in 1648 but quickly surrendered when attacked by General Lambert who called it 'Selby Castle' when reporting its capture. After the Restoration it was purchased by the Gilpins who made the S wing habitable, and in 1685 it was described as 'lately repaired and new modelled'. In 1741 it was purchased by Edward Stephenson who allowed it to decay, and by 1772 it was ruinous. Early in the 19c it was sold to Rowland Fawcett who restored the S block, and in 1814 the castle comprised 'a very ancient octagon tower, now much decayed, a high square tower, also in ruins, and a more modern castellated building, a comfortable residence'. In 1838 'some of the more modern portion' were 'being rebuilt in the Gothic style'. Sold to James Watt in 1944, it was   later acquired by Lord Henley. Occupied.

OMH pp.344-6; CE.2 pp.331-2; T.8(1908)pp.376-8, 26(1926)pp.398-413; CT pp.188, 235-7; BCP pp.169-70; CCW pp.163-5; OS.NY46SW/2.

SHANK   E2   NY 469704   83

A four-storey tower which stood on the W bank of the River Lyne, 16km NE of CARLISLE, was demolished 1951-2 because of its dangerous condition.

It was rectangular, 15.85 x 8.99m over walls 1.22-1.68m thick, and 12.19m high, with the main entrance in the NW wall at first floor level, 3.05m above ground level and probably reached by a wooden staircase. A door in the SW wall gave access to the ground floor which contained a circular staircase

giving access to the first floor. From here a circular staircase in the SW wall gave access to the upper floors. The interior of the tower was divided by two NW-SE cross walls.

Probably built c.1600, but was first mentioned as 'a neat house' in 1618 when occupied by Sir William Hutton, steward to the Earl of Cumberland, who resided here until 1622. It was ruinous and abandoned by 1777.

OMH p.351; CT p.395; T.22(1922)pp.162-8, 54(1954)pp.144-51; BCP p.170; OS.NY47SE/1.

SIZERGH   (W) E9   SD 499879   97

Situated on rising ground beside a tributary of the River Kent, 5km SSW of KENDAL, it dates mainly from c.mid-16c, with 18th and 19c alterations and additions, and incorporates a 14c towerhouse. There are traces of a surrounding ditch.

The towerhouse and attached hall block form the S end, with two-storey wings to the S and N, and a modern wall closing the W end of the courtyard, which measures 29 x 32m. The four-storey towerhouse (2) 10.67 x 18.59m, is 17.68m high, with walls of plain rubble, 3.05m thick at base reducing to 1.68m above. A newel staircase in the E wall gives access to all floors and to the roof where it terminates in a turret. Another turret projecting from the W wall contains small rooms which com-

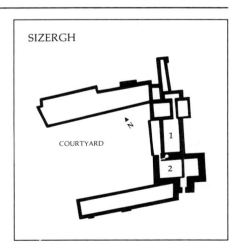

municate with the main floors.

The towerhouse was probably built c.1340 by Sir Walter Strickland (died

Scaleby Castle: the entrance.

c.1362) and altered in 1749. The hall range (1) was rebuilt by both Sir Walter Strickland (died 1569) and his widow, who later married Sir Thomas Boynton, and more alterations and additions were made in the 18c. In 1898 the lower part of the S centre portion was removed, and replaced by a carriageway to the courtyard. The N and S wings, 41 x 6m and 38 x 6m respectively, were added later in the 16c by Sir Walter's son. The castle was abandoned in 1641 for the duration of the Civil War, the Parliamentary generals issuing 'safe conduct' documents to protect it from 'plunder and confiscation'. It was again abandoned between 1687-99, possibly because it was ruinous, but has since been occupied by successive generations of the Strickland family. NT. OTV. GA.

T.10(1888)pp.48-94, 25(1925)pp.355-61; OMH pp.182-98; CE.2 p.292; CL.19(1906)pp.942-50, 106(1944)pp.1216-18; CT pp.314-6; RC pp.105-8; BE pp.289-91; CCW pp.166-75; OS.SD48NE/1.

SMARDALE (W) G7 NY 739082 91

Remains of a possible motte and bailey situated immediately N of the 16c Smardale Hall, 3km W of Kirkby Stephen. It is sub-rectangular and almost completely surrounded by a ditch; aerial photographs show a possible triangular shaped motte against the old railway embankment.

Possibly founded by the de Smardales mentioned in 1202, and abandoned before c.1292 when the manor passed to the de Harclas.

Arch. J. 132 (1975) p.47; CFH p.406; OS.NY70NW/17.

TEBAY (W) F7 NY 61.05. 91

There are two motte and bailey sites in the Tebay area.

CASTLE HOWE 613051 ᴬᴹ

A fine motte and bailey situated between the River Lune and the northbound slip road of the M6, west of Tebay, 19km N of KENDAL.

It comprises a damaged motte isolated from the roughly U-shaped bailey to the S by a semi-circular ditch, c.6m wide and 2m deep. The motte, 5.79m high, originally had base and summit diameters of c.61 and 34m respectively, but only the S half survives with remains of a breastwork. The bailey, c.133 x 61m, and c.2m high above outside levels, has had its SE angle quarried away. There is no trace of a surrounding ditch.

It was possibly built in the 12c by the de Tybai or Tibbay family, Herbert de Tibbay and his son Richard being mentioned in 1201. This and the site below were reputedly used at a later date as batteries 'to oppose the inroads of the Scots'.

CT pp.32-3; RC p.225; OS.NY60NW/4

CASTLE HOWE
(Greenholme) 600054

Remains of what may be an unfinished motte and bailey situated at the confluence of the Dorothy and Birk becks, 1½km NW of CASTLE HOWE motte and bailey and ½km SE of Greenholme. The site is not good defensively as it is ove looked by higher ground on two sides.

In 1913 it was described as 'having the appearance of once being a motte and bailey. The motte would appear to have been situated in the angle formed by the steep bank sides, where the western bank boldly projects outwards in a semi-circular form. This corner is also the highest portion of the area, but the inner half of the mound is not defined by any intervening ditch'. The 'motte' is a low oval-shaped mound, its summit measuring c.23 x 9.14m, and isolated from the field to the E by a semi-circular shaped depression, possibly an unfinished ditch. A boundary wall crosses the motte from N to S.

CT p.29; RC p.225.

TRIERMAIN ᴬᴹ   F2   NY 595669   86

Situated beside the B.6318 road 4km W of Gilsland, it comprises a mound 49 x 55m, and 4m high, covered with fallen masonry, traces of foundations, and a portion of a probable 14c tower. The mound is formed from the end of a ridge by a N-S cross-ditch, 1.50m deep and 6.40m wide. The castle was quadrangular, c.22 x 21m, with a tower at the E and W ends, the latter a gatehouse which had 'The Vauxes' arms set in stone very ancient' above the entrance. The surviving portion of tower is the SE angle of the gatehouse, c.9.14m high, almost its full original height, which c.1925 was 'buttressed and preserved from further dilapidation through the care of the Earl of Carlisle'.

In 1340 Roland de Vaux received a licence to crenellate his dwelling at 'Trevermane', and between 1461-83 it passed by marriage to Sir Richard Salkeld. After his death in 1501 it passed to his daughters who by 1510 were in dispute with Thomas, Lord Dacre over its ownership, which the latter eventually won. It was probably abandoned after its forfeiture in 1569 because of the Dacres involvement in the rebellion, and by 1580 'Trivermain house or castle ... is all for the most part fallen down and decaid, the repairing... where with help of the stones of the old building and the wood belonging to the lord and owner of the same is estimated to £300 beside the new casting of the moat which until a greater necessity may be spared'. By 1588 'Tradermayne castle' was 'utterly decayed', and in 1599, when it was called 'Tridermaine', it was described as 'an old castle'. One of the surviving towers was removed c.1688, and in 1832 a greater part of what remained collapsed, the materials being used in adjacent farm buildings.

T.3(1876-7)pp.175-8, 26(1926)pp.247-54; OMH p.349; CE.2 pp.332-3; CT pp.189, 238-40; CCW pp.179-80; OS.NY56NE/2.

WESTNEWTON ^{AM} B4 NY 130437 85

Shown as a motte on old OS maps, the slight earthworks are probably those of a fortified manor house, possibly of the de Newtons who held the manor from c.1130 until the period 1327-77. Situated on low-lying ground at the W end of the village, 2¼km NNW of ASPATRIA, it has no known history. It comprises earthworks of an inner enclosure (1), 40 x 28m, with possible tower mounds (2), at the western angles, both 1.37m high, and 21.34 x 16.76m in diameter. To the W is an outer enclosure, 58 x 73m indicated by scarps and ditches, and to the SE possible traces of another enclosure indicated by a ditch and containing a small mound (3).

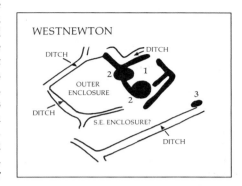

CFH p.243; OS.NY14SW/4.

WHELP (W) F5 NY 637256 91
Called CASTELLUM WELP 1199-1225, WHEALLEP 1590 and WELLOP 1750.

(Castellrig, a field name near Kirkby Thore, mentioned between c.1179-1294, may have a connection.)

There are no visible remains of the castle reputedly built by a person called Whelp 'from ruins of the Roman fort [of Bravoniacum at Kirkby Thore] in the first half of the 12c'. It stood inside the fort and a 12c grant of land by Alan, son of Roland, Lord of Galloway to John de Newbigging, refers to the 'tofts and crofts which are between castellum Welp and the mill'. It had been abandoned by the 15c when masonry from the castle was used to build the nearby Kirkby Thore Hall, and more masonry was removed between 1676-9 to build the first stone bridge over the Troutbeck (demolished c.1837), replacing an earlier one.

NB 1 p.379; T.2(1875-6)p.246, 17(1917)p.228; RNW pp.153, 157; PNW.2 pp.118-9; OS.NY62NW/19.

WOLSTY ^{AM} B4 NY 104506 85
Called WRISTIE 1563-6, WOOLSTEY 1636, ULSTEY, VLSTEY.

A rectangular moated site situated on low ground in a bend of a stream, 1km E of the Solway shore, and comprising a mound c.27 x 31m, surrounded by a moat, c.1m deep and 8.23m-16.76m wide. Two large blocks of fallen masonry survive and the summit is covered by grass-covered foundations of buildings.

The abbots of Holme Cultram had erected a building here by c.1327, probably the manor house of 'Wolmsty' for which a licence to crenellate was issued in 1348, and used not only for defence but also 'for a treasury and place of surety to lay up their books, charters and evidences against the sudden invasion of the Scottish'. From this time until the 17c it was in the care of the Chambers family. At the Dissolution it passed to the Crown and was then described as being 'in a good state and used for the defence of the inhabitants thereabouts'. By 1572 however, it was 'ruinous and decayed in all the houses within the outer wall' which comprised 'the hall with a chamber attached, the Evidence house, the kitchen, the peathouse, byer and the stable'. A survey describing it as 'partly decayed' in 1580 adds 'that this house or castle belongs to Her Majesty, it's keeper, Thomas Chambers should repair it'. In 1581 the local inhabitants offered to repair it at their own cost, but their offer was apparently refused, for in 1583 it was granted to Robert Chamber 'with the fee of 20 shillings yearly, for the keeping thereof'. The fee was not enough and the Chambers family spent much of their own money on repairs and continued to live here until c.1641 when it passed by marriage to Thomas Barwis (died 1648). It apparently suffered damage during the Civil War as it was ruinous in 1649, and in 1652 was demolished on the orders of Thomas Fitch, Governor of Carlisle and the materials taken to Carlisle, though some were used to build a house at Hayrigg 2km E at GR.126507. A list of the buildings demolished, compiled in 1654, mentions 'The Hall, one tower at the end of the Hall, one great barn, one Larder House, one long gallery, one chapel with a chamber at the end, one chamber called Michael Scots chamber, one house called the prison, one tower above the said house, one long byer, and one great stable', it also refers to 'the ruins of the walls of the castle' (Michael Scot was a wizard born c.1175 and died c.1235, and his chamber reputedly housed his books of spells etc.). By 1913 the only visible masonry surviving was 'a large block lying on the northern side' of the curtain wall 'at least 7 feet in thickness'.

T.1 (1901)pp.194-207; 11(1911)pp.235-40, 21(1921)p.103; CT pp.189, 241-3; CE.2 p.333; Register of Holme Cultram. F. Grainger and W. Collingwood (1929)p.135; HKW.3 pt.1 p.230; OS. NY15SW/5.

WORKINGTON HALL   A5   NY 008288   89

The shell of this fortified manor house, consolidated and well maintained, occupies a steep sided knoll above the S bank of the River Derwent on the E side of the town. It dates mainly from the 16c with later additions, but incorporates a 14c towerhouse and its 15c additions.

As originally built it probably comprised the towerhouse (1) and its buildings forming the E end, with walls or palisades extending W to join rectangular shaped towers flanking the entrance at the W end (2). The three-storey towerhouse 13.11 x 10.36m over walls 2.13-2.74m thick, had its upper parts rebuilt between 1782-1828. The L-shaped hall (3) 18.29 x 12.19m, and kitchen block (4) 18.90 x 7.93m, attached to the N and E sides were added c.1540, replacing an earlier hall of c.1404. Two wings (5 and 6) along the N and S sides added c.1597 transformed the fortress into a mansion, and there were further alterations and additions between 1782-1828.

Patrick de Culwin reputedly acquired the manor between 1199-1216 and moved here, probably from 'Burrow Walls', a possible fortified tower situated 1km NNW at GR.003301. In 1380 Gilbert de Curwen IV received a licence to crenellate his 'house at Wyrkyngton', referred to as 'the castle of Wyrkyngton' in 1402. In 1568 Sir Henry Curwen gave refuge at Workington, probably at the hall, to Mary, Queen of Scots when she landed here on her flight from Scotland. It remained with the Curwens until c.1930 when it passed by marriage to the Chance family. Presented to the town in 1946 it was neglected and allowed to decay, and later the upper parts were demolished.

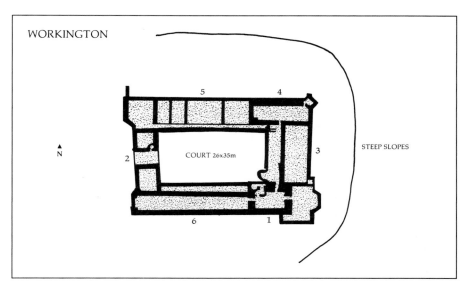

T.16(1899-1900)pp.1-15; CT pp.190, 244-7; CCW pp.185-7; OS.NY02NW/1.

WYTHOP   C5   NY 202284   89/90

Wythop Hall, dating from 1673, and situated 8¾km ESE of COCKER-MOUTH, may stand on the site of Hugh de Lowther's 'house at Wythe-hope', for which he received a licence to crenellate in 1318. Possibly rebuilt c.mid 16c., it was described as 'ruinated' in 1671, and though rebuilt in 1678 it does not incorporate any earlier work. There are no traces of outworks.

OMH pp.324-5; CT pp.45,188; PNC.2 p.457; CCW pp.187-8.

Brough Castle: the keep.

APPENDIX

The following are a list of 'castle' place names, etc., and include buildings, hill-forts, camps, etc., field names, and earthworks previously considered to be castle sites but which later documentary evidence and/or excavation have proved otherwise.

AM = Ancient Monument; FN = Field Name; IA = Iron Age; IAHF = Iron Age Hill Fort; PN = Place Name.

Aikton Castle	NY548380 90. Or Little Salkeld Castle. Turf covered foundations of a substantial building. LW p.271; OS.NY53NW/8.
Augill Castle	NY805138 82. 19c castellated mansion. M p.146; BE p.232; HKS pp.19-20.
Averell Castle	NY482222 90. PN first mention 1588. Possibly refers to the stone circle here. PNW.2 p.215.
Beetham Hall	SO499791 97. Towerhouse sometimes called a castle. RC pp.40-1; T.4(1904) pp.225-32; CCW pp.37-8.
Birch Castle	NY556607 86. Modern house.
Brown Castle	NY863134 92. A rocky scar. PNW.2 p.75.
Buck Castle	NY325224 89/90. Rocky crags on Matterdale Common. PNC.2 p.316.
Castilowe	NY46.23. 90. PN mentioned 1578, possibly referring to the homestead moat 'Trostremont' at GR 467236. PNW.2 p.215.
Castle, The (Askham)	NY472204 90. PN on Halton Fell. Castle Side is another PN ¼km SSE. PNW.2 p.201.
Castle Bank (Brampton)	NY525629 86. A small knoll.
Castle Bank (Grayrigg)	SD581964 90/97. Or Castley Bank, a farmhouse. Castle Fell is a PN at GR.570014.
Castle Banks (Little Strickland)	NY56.19. 90. FN possibly associated with some earthworks at GR.561198. PNW.2 p.152; RC p.222.
Castleber	NY741168 91. PN near Warcop. PNW.2 p.84.
Castle Carrock (Hallsteads)	NY545551 86. Suggested alternative site of Castle Carrock Castle. Earthworks here are natural. OS.NY55NW/7.
Castle Cleugh	NY55.86. 80. Nether and Upper Castle Cleugh are PNs on the Bewcastle Fells.
Castle Colby	NY648212 91. PN adjacent to Bewley Castle mentioned in 1851. M p.232.
Castle Crag (Borrowdale)	AM. NY249159 89/90. Possible IAHF. T.23(1923) p.252, 24(1924) p.83; OS.NY21NW/2; LPTT.1 p.122.
Castle Crag (Kentmere)	NY445052 90. Rocky crag.
Castle Crag (Wythburn)	NY305119 90. Rocky crag.

Castle Dubdale (Shap) | NY56.15. 91. FN 'on a precipice at the Churn, in Shap Rural'. PNW.2 p.179.

Castledyke, Low | NY544448 86. PN called Castledike in 1568. PNC.1 p.170.

Castle Farm (Hardendale) | NY58.14. 91. PN 2km SE of Shap church and Castlehowe Scar is a PN 1km N. PNW.2 p.158; SBD p.316.

Castle Farm (Low Hesket) | NY467463 86. PN 2km W of Castle Hewin.

Castlefield (Beckfoot) | NY09.48. 85. FN Eight fields containing site of Bibra Roman fort, once locally called 'Mawbray Castle'. A land division agreement made c1767 is titled 'Articles of Division for Newton Castle', which may allude to WESTNEWTON or the nearby hamlet of Newton. T.4(1878-9) pp.318-20, 5(1880-1) pp.137-8; Carlisle Patriot & Journal 14.11.1879.

Castlefield (Walton) | NY535643 86. FN contains site of Roman milecastle 55.

Castle Folds (Asby) | AM. NY649093 91. Or Castlesteads. A possible medieval defensive site. RC pp.19-20; T.33(1933) pp.233-7.

Castle Head (Grange) | SD421797 97. Or Atterpile Castle. A promontory fort. T.1(1901) pp.315-6; OS.SD47NW/1; FCN p.31.

Castle Head (Keswick) | NY271228 89/90. PN. NT. OTV. Castlerigg Hall GR.283225 modern house with c.mid17c woodwork.

Castle Hewin | NY485463 86. Called Castelewyn in 1272. No visible remains. Probably a circular univallate hill-fort. CT pp.263-4; T.9(1909) pp.209-12; LW p.225.

Castle Hill (Boothby) | NY544630 86. FN contains site of a Roman fort. T.34(1934) pp.154-5; OS.NY56SW/14.

Castle Hill (Cumwhitton) | NY496511 86. Ploughed down defensive earthwork. OS. NY45SE/11.

Castle Hill (Dufton) | AM. NY702230 91. Circular hill-fort or homestead. RC pp.94-5; BHF p.140.

Castle Hill (Kirklinton) | NY432674 85. Supposed site of Kirklinton Castle, probably site of a tower. T.10(1910) p.107, 11(1911) p.44, 12(1912) pp.59-75.

Castlehill Wood (Near Sawrey) | SD371957 97. PN. Castle Farm is opposite and there is a modern house called 'The Castle' adjacent.

Castle How (Ennerdale) | NY091163 89. PN. T.25(1925) p.135.

Castle How (Grasmere) | NY308077 90. Or Castle Crag, and Great and Little Castle How are nearby. PNW.1 p.199; T.28(1928) p.285.

Castle How (Harter Fell) | NY237004 89/90. Rectangular enclosure and other earthworks. T.18(1918) pp.97,238; ASC p.39, and Maiden Castle c.GR.22.99 is a supposed hill-fort. T.23(1923) p.271; ASC p.55.

Castle How (Little Langdale) | NY297033 90. Small rocky hill.

Castle How (Old Hutton) | SD56.88. 97. FN. PNW.1 p.129.

Castle How (Orton)	NY62.08. 91. PN on 1859 6" OS map. Called Castle Folds in 1777. Remains of a sheep fold here. PNW.2 p.45.
Castle How (Peel Wyke/ Wythop)	AM. NY201308 89/90. IA promontory fort. T.11(1911) pp. 118-21, 24(1924) pp.78-87.
Castlehow (Shap)	NY579089 91. PN possibly taking its name from IAHF at GR.577096. Arch.J.132(1975) pp.49,51.
Castle How (Uldale)	NY258342 89/90. PN possibly from John de Kaystre/Castre here in 15c or moated site at GR.248344. PNC.2 p.328; T.6(1881-2) p.511.
Castle How (Ulpha)	SD190921 96. Rocky outcrop. ASC p.55.
Castle Knott (Middleton Fells)	SD657842 97. Probable boundary cairn 537m above sea level. PNW.1 p.25.
Castle Neb (Windermere)	SD c.41.99. 90. PN on 1859 OS map. PNW.1 p.195.
Castlerigg (Lazonby Fell)	NY504415 86. Farmhouse, moated building here c.1794. H.1. p.289. OS.NY54SW/10. Maiden Castle AM, 1½km SW GR.502404, is a village settlement. OS.NY54SW/5.
Castle Rock (St John's)	NY321197 89/90. Or Castle Rock of Triermain, and in 1278 Castelyndolf/Casteliadolf. Enclosure and traces of a building of 'indeterminate date'. T.16(1916) pp.224-9; PNC.2 p.316. Ing Castell is a FN in the parish. PNC.2 p.319. Round Castle PN in the parish is 'round castell' in 1604, Round Castle in 1739 and shown as 'Round Mount' on 6" OS map. PNC.2 p.317.
Castleshields	NY438583 85. Farm near Linstock.
Castelskua	NY68.19. 91. Called Castlescugh 1649, Castleskews 1740. PN near Appleby alluding to woodlands owned by the castle. PNW.2 p.99.
Castle Slack (Ouseby)	NY622352 91. PN mentioned 1236-9 'the dyke of Castelslack'. Perhaps associated with the moated site at Crewgarth GR.601349. T.8(1886) p.66, 30(1930) pp.9, 132-6; PNC.1 p.229; LW p.259; OS.NY63SW/3.
Castlesteads (Anthorn)	NY170584 85. FN possibly site of medieval watch tower built over Roman milecastle No.5. OS.NY15NE/5.
Castlesteads (Dalston)	NY392450 90. Earthworks, possibly Roman or a village site. OS.NY34NE/5; PNC.1 p.137; H.1. pp432-3; T.81(1981) pp.1-6. Castlesteads, High/Low FNs 'nearer to Brackenshaw' GR.37.48. T.10(1888) p.264; PNC.1 p.248.
Castlesteads (Natland)	AM. SD530888 97. IAHF. RC pp.181-2; T.8(1908) pp.108-12.
Castlesteads (Pardshaw)	NY10.25. 89. Site of 'the earthen ring of a British enclosure'. T.3(1876-7) pp.343-4.
Castlesteads (Plumpton)	NY493385 90. Farmhouse on site of Voreda Roman Fort. Called La Castellstede 1597, Castleshields 1750, Castle-Steeds 1777. Fort called Plumpton Castle in late 17c. PNC.1 p.234.
Castlesteads (Walton)	NY511633 86. Late 18c mansion. BE. p.196; CE.2 p.303.

Castlesteads (Yanwath)

AM. NY519252 90. Possible Iron Age defended settlement. RC p.253; T3(1876-7) p.252; OS.NY52NW/31.

Castle Tower (Dallam)

SD493808 97. IAHF on Castle Hill, called Castle Tower by late 17c. RC p.104; OS.SD48SE/3.

Castling (Birkby)

NY06.37. 89. FN 'there are two fields called Castling i.e. the Castle meadow — under the shadow of Paper Hill'. Article on field name in and around Maryport in West Cumberland Times Feb. 12th and 19th (1910).

Catcastle (Kendal)

SD51.92. 97. PN used between 1767-1864. T.8(1908) p.100.

Cobra Castle (Egremont)

NY025117 89. A farmhouse.

Collinsons Castle

NY459379 90. Site of 'ancient square fortification'. No visible remains. H.1. p.512; T.10(1910) pp.115-6.

Croglam Castle

AM. NY768076 91. IA univallate enclosure, similar to Castle Hill (Dufton) and Waitby. RC. p.143; HKS p.10; OS.NY70NE/ 3.

Denton

NY57.63 86. Earthworks at Denton Hall GR.579631, and Upper Denton GR.615655 were once considered to be motte and bailey sites. T.6(1881-2) p.194; CT. pp.22,28; OS.NY56SE/ 8 and NY66NW/2.

Dovenby Hall

NY094334 89. A possible 12c tower incorporated into Dovenby Hall, thought to be part of a Norman castle. There are three mounds in the grounds of the hall. T.23(1923) p.248; NCB p.169; BE p.78; OS.NY03SE/7.

Drawdykes Castle

NY418586 85. 17c tower on earlier site. H.2 p.581; CT p.368; OS.NY45NW/8; T.12(1912) pp.194-200, 22(1922) pp.452-3; BCP pp.81-2; CCW pp.83-4; GM.103 pt.1 (1833) p.104.

Dunmallet/Dunmallard Castle

AM. NY468246 90. IAHF. T.1(1866-73) pp.157-9, 3(1878) p.248; Arch.J.132(1975) p.36.

Dunwalloght Castle

NY559502 86. Ploughed out site, no coherent plan visible. Possible settlement site. T.9(1909) pp.218-21; NB p.511.

Edmond Castle

NY498586 86. Large early 19c mansion. Emount Castle was a PN here in 1620. T.8(1908) p.16; BE p.137.

Forceknott Castle

NY562381 90. PN at Eden Lacy c.1800 when the last remains of 'Force Knott Castle' were 'carted off'. T.13(1913) p.172-3, 25(1925) p.117.

Frizington

NY04.15. 89. A suggested motte here was probably a spoil mound. CT p.39; T.23(1923) p.258.

Gill Castle (Crosby Garrett)

NY72.09. 91. FN. PNW.2 p.41.

Green Castle (Dunfell)

NY712311 91. PN and site of circular enclosure. NB.1 p.388; PNW.2 p.122.

Greencastle (Alston)

NY699398 91. Farmhouse. H.1. p.263; OS.NY63NE/2.

Greeny Castle (Dean)

NY072251 89. Or Green. Earthworks in Glebe Field are reputedly those of a castle, but are probably archery butts or spoil heaps. T.3(1876-7) p.345, 23(1923) p.34; PNC.2 p.368; OS.NY02NE/11.

Hallbankgate	NY581594 86. Mound, suggested as a motte, is a natural feature. OS.NY55NE/5.
Hardcastle (Hindscarth)	NY216168 90. Cairn. Castle Nook is a PN 1½km ENE. T.3(1876-7) pp.244-8.
Hardknott Castle	AM. NY219015 89/90. Roman fort. T.12(1891-2) pp.228-33, 375-438, 28(1928) pp.314-39.
Haresceugh Castle	NY611421 86. Remains of possible tower overlooked by Castle Hill, a natural knoll. T.9(1909) pp.220-4.
Headswood Castle (Walton)	NY504632 86. Natural hill once considered to be motte and bailey site. CT p.40; OS.NY56SW/36.
Heights Castle (Ormside)	NY693152 91. 19c farmhouse. PNW.2 p.90.
High Cross Castle (Troutbeck)	SD404013 90. Large two-storey mansion, now a Youth Hostel. PNW.1 p.191. Castle How, GR.400017, is a FN nearby. PNW.1 p.191.
Hornby Castle (Ravenstonedale)	SD729969 98. Needle House was called Hornby Castle. PNW.2 p.39.
How, The	NY506563 86. Natural hill, wrongly suggested to have been adapted as a motte. T.6(1881-2) p.470; OS.NY55NW/1.
Hyndcastell (Hincaster)	SD51.84. 97. Village so called in 1544. PNW.1 p.89.
Lamplugh	NY088207 89. Small steep sided hillock behind Lamplugh Hall, wrongly suggested as possible motte. OMH p.338; CT p.292; OS.NY02SW/1.
Lazon Castle	NY500541 86. Also called Lazen, Glasson-Leyson 1589, Laysin 1603, Lasen 1613. Natural hill 4km SSW of Hayton. PNC.1 p.74; T.7(1907) p.43,50, 12(1912) p.200.
Lowther Castle	NY522239 90. Shell of 19c mansion. CT pp.300-2; BE p.272; T.81(1981) pp.122-36; 84(1984) pp.191-204; Architectural Drawings from Lowther Castle, ed. E. Colvin (1980); CCW pp.124-30; OMH pp.93-6.
Maborough Castle (Kirkby Thore)	NY63.25. 91. FN contains earthworks of probable E angle of Roman fort. PNW.2 p.119.
Maiden Castle (Low Abbey)	NY651272 91. PN shown on Greenwood's 1823 map. PNW.2 p.119.
Maiden Castle (Stainmore)	AM. NY372132 92. Roman fort. RC pp.215-6; PNW.2 p.71; T.5(1880-1) pp.69-75; 27(1927) pp.170-78. Possibly the "Mayden Castell" of 1292.
Maiden Castle (Wasdale)	NY184054 89/90. Site of a beacon; called Maiden Castle in 1587. T.3(1876-7) p.250; ASC p.34.
Maiden Castle (Watermillock/ Soulby)	AM. NY451243 90. Also called Caerthanock Camp, and is Mayden castell in 1285. Probable Iron Age settlement. T.1(1866-73) pp. 157-61, 12(1912) pp.143-5; PNC.1 pp.255-6; Arch. J. 132(1975) p.36; OS.NY42SE/3. Castlehows Point is a PN ¼km E of Watermillock. PNC.1 p.257. Castle Gate FN near Watermillock mentioned 1673. PNC.1 p.258.

Monk Castle	NY428461 85. Farmhouse, early OS maps erroneously call it 'Muncaster Castle'. T.10(1910) p.117.
Old Castle (Glenridding)	NY383161 90. Traces of an earthwork. PNW.2 p.226; OS.NY31NE/M.
Old Castle (Triermain)	NY584678 86. PN. NE of Moorguards Farm. OS.NY56NE/M.
Palmcastel	NY26.46. 85. Called Palmcastell 1272, Palmcastre 1305, Palme Castell 1578. An enclosure of c.23 hectares, part of which contains Old Carlisle Roman fort. The Antiquary 41(1905) pp.409-11; PNC.2 p.330.
Pennington	SD264774 96. A mound once considered to be a motte, but more probably a spoil mound. Scheduled as AM as 'Burial Mound'. T.6(1906) p.317; AME p.130; OS.SD27NE/19.
Popes Castle (Cockermouth)	NY12.30. 89. House name mentioned 1737. T.23(1923) p.73.
Raby Castle (Shap)	NY53.14. 91. c.1904 a field called 'Raby', near Tailbert Farm, contained 'traces of Raby Castle'. SBD p.330; OS.NY51SW/4.
Ratten Castle (Sowerby Row)	NY391408 90. Farmhouse.
Rattenby Castle (St Bees)	NY97.11. 89. PN mentioned 1794. PNC2 p.432; H.2 p.35.
Reecastle	NY275175 89/90. Supposed site of IAHF is in fact a natural feature. T.24(1924) p.83; BE p.73; OS.NY21NE/4.
Roper Castle	AM. NY882112 92. Roman signal station. RC p.217; HKS p.25.
Rose Castle (Hawkshead)	SD333999 96. PN.
Ross Castle	NY384634 85. Modern farmhouse.
St Mungo's Castle	AM. NY176470 85. Or Mungo Castle; Bromfield Camp. A damaged homestead moat. Probably the 'Curia [court] de Bromfield' mentioned in 1227. T.4(1904) p.347, 25(1925) p.348.
Sebergham Castle	NY330433 85. Late 18c mansion. BE p.188; T.12(1912) p.201; Sale Particulars CRO SX/132 1899; Whellan p.250.
Shoulthwaite Castle	AM. NY299188 89/90. IAHF. LPTT.2 p.122; OS.NY21NE/2.
Starling Castle	NY012045 89. Modern house. T.47(1947) p.219.
Stonehaugh Tower	NY462803 79. Towerhouse sometimes called a castle. T.9 (1909) pp.216-7.
Tarn Castle (Wigton)	NY25.51. 85. A building (destroyed) which stood on a hill S of Martin Tarn. History of Wigton — T.W. Carrick (1949) p.239.
Toppin Castle (Hayton)	NY497571 86. Castellated tower built c.1861 on site of 'Toppins Castle', a cottage mentioned 1790. A 'Typping Castle' is mentioned c.1540. PNC.1 p.90; T.12(1912) pp.200-1; Bulmer (1901) p.202.
Waitby Castle (Kirkby Stephen)	AM. NY758082 91. Or Carnick Castle. A hill-fort or settlement. RC p.234; OS.NY70NE/4.

Walls Castle (Ravenglass)

AM. SD088960 96. Remains of a Roman bath-house. T.3 (1876-7) pp.23-6, 28(1928) p.358-60; PNC.2 p.426; ASLD pp.46-7.

Whitehaven Castle

NX978179 89. Large mansion, converted 1926 into a hospital. Wh. p.440; T.3(1876-7) pp.362-3, 9(1888) p.345; TAMS.28 (1984) pp.61-92.

Wray Castle (Ambleside)

SD373009 96/97. 19c mansion. BE(N.Lancs) p.265; Hawkshead, H.S.Cowper (1899) p.41.

Yewfield Castle

SD35.99. 96. PN. T.9(1888) pp.152, 159, 23(1923) pp.138-41; Archaeologia 53(1891) p.535.

Yoadcastle (Ulpha)

SD157952 97. PN.

Dacre Castle, a towerhouse built c1350.

Carlisle Castle, dominated by its massive keep.

The remains of Wolsty Castle, near the Solway shores.

CHRONOLOGY

WILLIAM I 1066-87

1066   William the Conqueror lands at Pevensey in Sussex, 29 September 1066. Battle of Hastings 14 October 1066. William crowned at Westminster Abbey 25 December.

1069   William's devastation of the northern shires.

1069   Gospatric (often referred to as Earl of Northumberland, though there is no charter evidence for the use of the title) placed in charge of the administration of most of Cumberland.

1070   Malcolm, King of Scotland invades Teesdale via Cumberland. Gospatric invades Cumberland.

1072   Gospatric, deprived of his authority, flees to Scotland where he is created Earl of Dunbar.

1086   Domesday Survey, Cumberland omitted because it was not yet part of England.

WILLIAM II 1087-1100 (third son of William I)

1092   William annexes Cumberland and Westmorland from Scotland and commences colonising with people from other parts of England. (The area annexed had been part of Scotland since AD945 when it was seized from Dunmail, King of Cumberland.) Most of Cumberland (at this time called 'The land of Carlisle') granted to Ranulf le Meschin who had married the king's niece and was a relative of the earl of Chester. Castles founded at Carlisle, Bewcastle, Brough and Liddel.

1093   November 13. First battle of Alnwick, provoked by William's seizure of Cumberland and Westmorland. King Malcolm and his son Edward killed. Expansion of Norman influence into Scotland.

HENRY I 1100-35 (fourth son of William I)

1120   Prince William, heir to the throne, drowned in the 'White Ship' disaster, so creating a disputed succession. Ranulf le Meschin succeeds to the earldom of Chester and surrenders Cumberland to the king.

1122   Henry visits Carlisle.

1130   Counties of Carlisle and Westmorland first recorded.

STEPHEN 1135-54 (nephew of Henry I)

1135   Stephen, Count of Boulogne, seizes the throne; commencement of civil war (The Anarchy) with Matilda, daughter of Henry I.

1136   King David invades England and takes Carlisle. First Treaty of Durham, much of Cumberland, Westmorland and Northumberland ceded to the Scots.

1138   King David invades into Yorkshire and is defeated near Northallerton September 22 (the Battle of the Standard); Egremont Castle and the surrounding area attacked by William fitz Duncan.

1139   Second Treaty of Durham. Prince Henry of Scotland has the lands granted to his father in 1136 confirmed to him, also created earl of Northumberland which included an administrative area of Cumberland, Durham, Lancashire north of the Ribble, and Westmorland.

| 1153 | End of Civil War. Stephen orders the demolition of adulterine castles, a process completed by Henry II. King David dies at Carlisle. |

HENRY II 1154-89 (son of Matilda, daughter of Henry I)

1157	Treaty of Chester. All land ceded to the Scots in 1136 surrendered to King Henry by King Malcolm.
1158	Henry and Malcolm meet at Carlisle. Hubert de Vaux granted the barony of Gilsland.
1165	King Malcolm dies and is succeeded by his brother William (the Lion).
1170	Henry, second son of Henry II crowned 14 June 1170 (d.1183). Certain chroniclers call him Henry III.
1173	Carlisle besieged by the Scots. The castles of Appleby, Brough, Brougham and possibly Pendragon confiscated from Hugh de Morville, participant in the murder of Archbishop Thomas Becket of Canterbury on 29 December 1170. The confiscations are often attributed to his involvement in the murder, but the real reason was for aiding and abetting the king's son Henry, in his rebellion.
1174	Liddle, Appleby and Brough castles taken by King William. Carlisle besieged. Second battle of Alnwick 13 June, King William captured and later released with conditions, one of which was the surrender of Berwick-upon-Tweed town and castle to the English Crown.
1177	County of Carlisle renamed County of Cumberland. The county of Westmorland formed from the baronies of Appleby and Kendal, and part of Yorkshire.

RICHARD I 1189-99 (third son of Henry II)

| 1189 | Richard frees King William of Scotland from his allegiance and subjugation to the Crown of England on payment of 10,000 marks. |

JOHN 1199-1216 (fifth son of Henry II)

1201	May. L to C issued for Kirkoswald.
1215	Magna Carta.
1215-17	First Barons War.
1216	Carlisle city and castle taken by the Scots.

HENRY III 1216-72 (son of John)

| 1237 | Treaty of York helps to stabilize the Borders for nearly fifty years. Alexander II resigns his hereditary claim to Cumberland and Westmorland, and is granted the manors of Carlatton, Langwathby, Salkeld, Scotby and Sowerby, and lands in Northumberland. |
| 1264-7 | Second Barons War. |

EDWARD I 1272-1307 (son of Henry III)

| 1280 | Edward's first visit to Carlisle. |
| 1286 | King Alexander III dies and is succeeded by his grand-daughter Margaret the 'Maid of Norway'. Edward confiscates all the manors granted to the Scots in 1237. |

1290	Margaret dies leaving the Scottish throne disputed by thirteen competitors.
1292	John Balliol elected King of Scotland by the adjudication of Edward.
1296	Balliol invades Cumbria, Carlisle besieged by John Comyn, Earl of Buchan. Balliol defeated at the Battle of Dunbar and abdicates. He is held prisoner in London and Edward takes the government of Scotland into his own hands.
1297	William Wallace invades north Cumberland.
1298	William Wallace defeated at the Battle of Falkirk.
1305	William Wallace captured and executed.
1306	Robert Bruce crowned King of Scotland as King Robert I, 25 March. He unifies Scots.
1307	20 January. Parliament meets at Carlisle. Edward dies at Burgh by Sands, 7 July.

EDWARD II 1307-27 (son of Edward I)

1307	August. Ls to C issued for Dunmalloght, Drumburgh and Scaleby.
1309	July. Ls to C issued for Brougham and Pendragon.
1314	Rose Castle taken by Scots under Edward Bruce who also burned Kirkoswald Castle. Battle of Bannockburn, Robert I defeats English and secures Scottish independence.
1315	Robert I invades Cumberland and unsuccessfully besieges Carlisle between 14 July and 3 August.
1316-18	Scaleby Castle destroyed or badly damaged by Scots who invade into Lancashire.
1318	July. L to C issued for Wythop Hall.
1319	Scots led by Black Douglas invade as far as Shap.
1322	Robert I invades as far as Lancaster. Defeats English at Byland (Yorkshire). Rose Castle burnt. March. L to C issued for Hayes. Andrew de Harcla created 1st Earl of Carlisle, 25 March.
1323	3 March. Andrew de Harcla forfeits earldom, which remained in abeyance until 1622, and is executed for treason. A thirteen year truce with the Scots agreed. Also agreed that no new fortifications be erected in Cumberland.
1327	Edward deposed 20 January. Robert I invades Cumberland.

EDWARD III 1327-77 (son of Edward II)

1327	Edward's accession 25 January. L to C issued for Piel. 21 September. Edward II murdered at Berkeley Castle (Gloucestershire).
1328	Peace agreement signed at York.
1329	Robert I dies and is succeeded by his son David II.
1330	Edward assumes personal rule.
1333	Scots led by Lord Archibald Douglas invade Cumberland. Scots defeated at the Battle of Halidon Hill.
1335	Ls to C issued for Naworth, July, and Millom, August.

1336	April. L to C issued for Rose.
1337	Scots invade northern Cumberland and burn Rose Castle.
1340	February. L to C issued for Triermain.
1341	Pendragon Castle burnt by the Scots.
1342	October. L to C issued for Highhead. Penrith town burnt by Scots.
1345	Scots, led by Sir William Douglas, invade Cumberland, Penrith town burnt and Gilsland wasted.
1346	Scots invade and capture Liddel Strength. Scots defeated at Nevilles Cross, King David II captured. April. L to C issued for Penrith town.
1348	Black Death. October. L to C issued for Wolsty.
1353	October. Ls to C issued for Greystoke and Hartley.
1355	June. L to C issued for Rose. Scots invade Cumberland.
1357	King David released from captivity.
1376	Death of Edward, the Black Prince, heir to the throne.

RICHARD II 1377-99 (son of the Black Prince)

1380	Scots invade Cumberland. L to C issued for Workington.
c.1382	Guns first appear in Cumberland.
1383	Scots attack Penrith.
1385	Scots and French combine to invade Cumberland.
1387	Scots take and burn Cockermouth Castle.
1388	Battle of Otterburn. Scots defeat the English. The English and Scottish kings agree that no new fortification shall be built or repaired in Cumberland except those in the process of being built.
1397	February. L to C issued for Penrith Castle, Ralph de Nevill created first Earl of Westmorland 29 September 1397.
1399	Richard is deposed by Henry, Duke of Lancaster, who ascends the throne as Henry IV, 30 September. April. L to C issued for Penrith Castle.

HENRY IV 1400-13 (son of John of Gaunt)

1402	Scots defeated at Hamildon Hill.
1406	King James I of Scotland captured at sea by English merchants and is held in captivity until 1424.

HENRY V 1413-22 (son of Henry IV)

HENRY VI 1422-61 (son of Henry V)

1424	King James I of Scotland released (see 1406).

1455	Commencement of the Wars of the Roses.
1461	Scots burn suburbs of Carlisle. Henry deposed.

EDWARD IV 1461-83 (eldest son of Richard, Duke of York)

1461	Death of Lord Clifford at the Battle of Towton. Richard, Duke of Gloucester, appointed Warden of the West March, makes additions to Bewcastle and Penrith castles.
1464	Battles of Hedgeley Moor, near Wooler 25 April, and Hexham 15 May, both in Northumberland. King Henry VI captured.
1465	Fifteen year truce agreed with the Scots.
1470	3 October Henry VI restored.
1471	11 April Henry VI deposed. Died 21 May.

EDWARD V 1483 (son of Edward IV)

RICHARD III 1483-85 (son of Richard, Duke of York)

1485	Battle of Bosworth. Richard killed. End of the Wars of the Roses, beginning of the Tudor period.

HENRY VII 1485-1509 (son of Edmund Tudor, Earl of Richmond)

1487	Lambert Simnel, Pretender to the English throne, lands at Piel Island, 4 June.

HENRY VIII 1509-47 (second son of Henry VII)

1513	Battle of Flodden, Scots defeated by Thomas Howard, Earl of Surrey. James IV of Scotland killed.
1525	Henry, Lord Clifford created first Earl of Cumberland 18 June. His descendants retain title until the death of Henry Clifford, the fifth Earl in 1643.
1528	Liddel Strength burnt by the Scots.
1536-9	Dissolution of the Monasteries.
1536	'Pilgrimage of Grace', a Northern rising due to political and religious grievances. Eight thousand rebels besiege Carlisle and are routed.
1536-43	John Leland, the King's antiquary, tours through England and Wales.
1537	Council of the North reconstituted to deal with the special problems of the border area. It was the judicial and administrative authority for the counties.
1542	Battle of Solway Moss, 24 November. English led by Sir Thomas Dacre and Jack Musgrave defeat the Scots.

EDWARD VI 1547-53 (son of Henry VIII)

1552	The 'Debateable Lands', an area of land north of Carlisle, disputed by the English and Scots, divided by a joint commission.

MARY I 1553-58 (daughter of Henry VIII)

ELIZABETH I 1558-1603 (second daughter of Henry VIII)

1561   Mary, Queen of Scots returns to Scotland from France.

1568   Mary flees to England, lands at Workington 17 May. Stays one night at Hayton Castle, then taken first to Cockermouth and then to Carlisle. Moved to Bolton Castle, Yorkshire, 13 July.

1569-70   'Rising of the North', known locally as 'Dacre's Raid', a rebellion led by the Earls of Northumberland and Westmorland, who demanded a return to Catholicism, etc. Appleby and Askerton castles partially dismantled.

1570   Another rising led by Leonard Dacre put down by Lord Hunsdon. Dacre's castles at Greystoke, Kirkoswald, Naworth and Rockcliffe confiscated.

1571   Charles Nevill, 6th Earl of Westmorland, forfeits the title.

1598   Plague ravages the counties.

JAMES I 1603-25 (was James VI of Scotland)

1603   Garrison at Carlisle reduced.

1617   The king visits Carlisle for three days.

1622   L to C issued for Millom. James Hay, Viscount Doncaster, created second Earl of Carlisle.

1624   Francis Fane created seventh Earl of Westmorland.

1627   Nearly 300 Scots invade as far as Penrith.

CHARLES I 1625-49 (son of James I)

1639   Carlisle re-garrisoned with 500 men.

1640   English defeated by Scots at Newburn-on-Tyne. Carlisle surrenders to Cromwell.

1641   Council of the North abolished. Garrison at Carlisle disbanded.

1642-8   Civil War.

1644   General Lesley besieges Carlisle.

1645   Carlisle surrenders, Scots garrison the castle.

1646   Scots depart.

1648   Carlisle taken by Royalists and garrisoned by the Scots. Cockermouth Castle besieged by the Royalists. Battle of Preston, Scots defeated.

OLIVER CROMWELL, Lord Protector 1653-8

RICHARD CROMWELL, Lord Protector 1658-9

CHARLES II 1660-85 (son of Charles I)

1660   Restoration of the Monarchy. Appleby, Brough, Brougham and Pendragon castles rebuilt and occupied by Anne Clifford, Countess of Pembroke.

1661   Charles Howard created fourth Earl of Carlisle.

JAMES II 1685-88 (second son of Charles I)

WILLIAM III 1689-1702 (son of William II Prince of Orange) and MARY 1689-94 (daughter of Charles I)

ANNE 1702-14 (daughter of James II)

1707   Union of England and Scotland.

GEORGE I 1714-27

1715   The 'Fifteen Rebellion' Jacobites, supporters of the Stewarts, invade and reach Preston. Defeated at the Battles of Preston and Sheriffmuir.

GEORGE II 1727-60 (son of George I)

1745   The 'Forty-five Rebellion'. Carlisle surrenders to the Jacobites led by Bonnie Prince Charlie 17 November. Scots retreat and Carlisle surrenders to the Duke of Cumberland, 30 December.

1746   Battle of Culloden, final defeat of the Jacobites by the Duke of Cumberland.

Penrith Castle

Bewley Castle, built in the 14th century by the Bishops of Carlisle.

SCOTTISH MONARCHS

Malcolm III (Canmore)	Son of King Duncan I	1058-93
Donald Bane	Brother of Malcolm. Deposed May 1094	1093-94
Duncan II	Son of Malcolm III	1094-94
Donald Bane	Restored November, 1094. Deposed 1097.	1094-97
Edgar	Son of Malcolm III	1097-1107
Alexander I	Son of Malcolm III	1107-24
David I	Son of Malcolm III	1124-53
Malcolm IV (The Maiden)	Son of Henry, son of David I	1153-65
William I (The Lion)	Brother of Malcolm IV. (Prisoner in England 1174-89)	1165-1214
Alexander II	Son of William I	1214-49
Alexander III	Son of Alexander II	1249-86
Margaret (Maid of Norway)	Grand-daughter of Alexander III. Her death left the throne disputed by thirteen competitors.	1286-90
John Balliol	Son of John de Balliol and Dervorguilla, great-great-grand-daughter of David I. Abdicated.	1292-96
Robert I (Bruce)	Great-grandson of second daughter of David, Earl of Huntingdon.	1306-29
David II	Son of Robert I. (Prisoner in England 1346-57)	1329-71
Edward Balliol	Son of John Balliol assumed title of King of Scotland. Crowned Sept. 1332, expelled Dec. 1332. Restored c.1333-36. Surrendered crown to Edward III of England 1356.	
Robert II (Stewart)	Son of Marjorie, daughter of Robert I.	1371-90
Robert III	Son of Robert II	1390-1406
James I	Son of Robert III. (Prisoner in England 1406-24)	1406-37
James II	Son of James I	1437-60
James III	Son of James II	1460-88
James IV	Son of James III	1488-1513
James V	Son of James IV	1513-42
Mary	Daughter of James V	1542-87
James VI	Son of Mary. Succeeded to the English Throne as James I, 24th March, 1603.	1567-1625

Brough Castle from the south-east.

BIBLIOGRAPHY

AF   *Antiquities of Furness.* T. West (1805).

AME   *Ancient Monuments in England,* 6th edn. (1973) HMSO.

Arch J   *Archaeological Journal** 1844-on.

ASC   *Archaeological Survey of Copeland.* G. Croford and C. George (1983).

ASLD   *Archaeological Sites of the Lake District.* T. Clare (1981).

BCP   *Borderland Castles and Peles.* R. Hugill (1970).

BE   *Buildings of England.* N. Pevsner.
          Cumberland and Westmorland (1967)
          North Lancashire (1969)

BHF   *British Hill-forts – An Index.* A.H.A. Hogg (1979).

BNC   *History of the Berwickshire Naturalists Club** 1832-on.

BN   *Proceedings of the Barrow Naturalists Field Club** (1877-1971).

Bulmer   *Bulmer's History and Directory of Cumberland* (1901).

CCA   *Churches, Castles and Ancient Halls of North Lancashire* Vol.1. W.O. Roper (1880).

CCW   *Castles of Cumberland and Westmorland.* R. Hugill (1977).

CE   *Castles of England.* Sir J.D. Mackenzie, 2 Vols (1897).

CFH   *Cumberland Families and Heraldry.* C. Roy Hudleston and R.S. Boumphrey (1978).

CG   *Chateau Gaillard, European Castle Studies.†* 1964-on.

CL   *Country Life Magazine** 1897-on.

CRO   Cumbria Record Office.

CT   *Castles and Fortified Towers of Cumberland, Westmorland and Lancashire North of the Sands.* J.F.
          Curwen (1913).

DAE   *Some Account of Domestic Architecture in England.* T.H. Turner and J.H. Parker, 4 Vols
          (1851-59).

EB   *English Baronies. A study of their origin and descent 1086-1327.* I.J. Sanders (1960).

EHR   *English Historical Review** 1886-on.

ENC   *Early Norman Castles of the British Isles.* E.S. Armitage (1912).

FCN   *Furness and Cartmel Notes.* H. Barber (1894).

GD   *The Gosforth District.* C.A. Parker (1904).

GM   *Gentleman's Magazine** (1731-1907).

H   *History of Cumberland.* W. Hutchinson, 2 Vols (1794) (reprint 1974).

HBC   *Handbook of British Chronology.* Royal Historic Society, 3rd Edn. (1986).

HKS   *Historic Kirkby Stephen and North Westmorland.* R. Sowerby, 2nd Edn. (1950).

HLC   *Handlist of English Royal Licences to Crenellate 1200-1578.* C. Coulson (forthcoming).

HKW	*History of the Kings Works.* Gen. Editor H.M. Colvin, 6 Vols (1963-82).
JBAA	*Journal of the British Archaeological Assn.** 1845-on.
LPTT	*Later Prehistory Trent to Tyne.* A.J. Challis and D.W. Harding, 2 Vols (1975).
LW	*History and Antiquities of Leith Ward.* S. Jefferson (1840).
M	*History, Topography and Directory of Westmorland.* Mannix and Co. (1851).
MA	*Medieval Archaeology** 1957-on.
MMA	*Medieval Military Architecture.* G.T. Clarke, 2 Vols (1884).
NB	*History and Antiquities of Cumberland and Westmorland.* J. Nicolson and R. Burn, 2 Vols (1777).
NCB	*Norman Castles in Britain.* D. Renn, 2nd Edn. (1973).
OMH	*The Old Manorial Halls of Westmorland and Cumberland.* M.W. Taylor (1892).
OS	Ordnance Survey Archaeological Reference Cards (constantly updated).
PNC	*Place Names of Cumberland.* English Place Name Society, 3 Vols (1971).
PNW	*Place Names of Westmorland.* English Place Name Society, 2 Vols (1967).
PSN	*Proceedings of the Society of Antiquaries of Newcastle** 1855-on.
RC	*Royal Commission of Historical and Ancient Monuments, Inventory for Westmorland.* HMSO (1936).
RNW	*Later Records of North Westmorland.* J. Curwen (1932).
RW	*The Roman Wall.* J.C. Bruce (1957).
SBD	*Shappe in Bygone Days.* J. Whiteside (1904).
SRW	*Memoir Written during a Survey of the Roman Wall.* H. Maclauchlan (1858).
T	*Transactions of the Cumberland and Westmorland Antiquarian and Archaeological Society**. Vols 1-16 (1866-1900) Old Series. New Series Vol 1 (1901-on).
TAMS	*Transactions of the Ancient Monument Society** 1953-on.
VCH	*Victoria County History* *Lancashire* 8 Vols (1906-14) *Yorkshire* Vol 2 (1912).
Wh	*History and Topography of Cumberland and Westmorland.* W. Whellan (1860).

*	regular series publication
†	irregular series publication

GLOSSARY

ADULTERINE   A castle erected without permission, mostly during the Anarchy of Stephen's reign.

ALIENATION   Transfer of ownership.

AM   Ancient Monument. Its preservation is considered to be of national importance.

ANARCHY   Term used to describe the Civil War of Stephen's reign (1135-54).

ASHLAR   Masonry cut to an even face and square edges.

BAILEY   A fortified enclosure forming part of a castle.

BARBICAN   An outer fortification defending the castle entrance.

BARMKIN   A defensive enclosure, usually attached to a towerhouse or bastle.

BARROW   Burial mound.

BARTIZAN   A parapet or a projecting gallery on a wall face. Term often used for a corbelled wall turret.

BASTION   A solid masonry projection from the general outline of a fortress from which flanking fire can be directed.

BASTLE   see PEEL/PELE

BELVEDERE   A building erected for the purpose of obtaining fine views, a summerhouse.

BERM   In earthworks, the flat space between a bank or curtain and the inner edge of its ditch or scarp.

BLOCKHOUSE   Small detached fort.

BIVALLATE   Defended by two concentric banks and ditches.

BRATTICE   A covered wooden gallery on a wall for the defence of its base, or a timber tower. Sometimes a temporary palisaded enclosure.

BREASTWORK   Bank protecting summit of mound or ringwork.

BRONZE AGE   The period from c.1600-600 B.C.

BULWARK   see BASTION

BURH   Saxon communal fortification.

BUTTERY   Room where wines, ales, etc., were kept.

BUTTRESS   Masonry built against a wall to give it additional support.

CAMERA   A vaulted room, a private chamber.

CAPITAL MESSUAGE   The main dwelling of the manor.

CAPITALS   Head or top part of a column.

CAPONIER   Covered passage within a ditch of a fort.

CASTELLAN   Person in charge of a castle.

CASTELLATED	Gaps in a parapet; see EMBRASURE.
CASTLE GUARD	see KNIGHTS FEE
CASTRUM, CASTELL	Old term for castle.
CLASPING BUTTRESS	Buttress encasing an angle.
CONFISCATE	Taken by the Crown as a penalty.
CONSTABLE	Official placed in charge of a castle when the owner was absent.
CORBEL	Block of stone projecting from a wall intended to support a weight.
COUNTERSCARP	Outer slope of a defensive ditch.
CRENELLATED	see CASTELLATED
CROSSWALL	A dividing wall.
CURTAIN WALL	The wall enclosing a courtyard or bailey, including any towers or bastions on it.
DECORATED	Architectural period c.1272-1377.
DISSOLUTION	Dissolution of the Monasteries 1536-40.
DOMESDAY	Domesday Book, the 1086 Norman survey of England.
DONJON	see KEEP
DRAWBRIDGE	Moveable bridge that can be raised towards a gateway by chains or ropes.
DRIPSTONE	Projecting moulding above an arch or lintel to throw off water.
DRYSTONE	Masonry built without mortar.
ELIZABETHAN	Architectural period during Queen Elizabeth I's reign, 1558-1603; see also TUDOR.
EH	English Heritage.
EMBRASURE	Opening in a parapet to allow archery or cannon to be used.
ENCEINTE	Main line of fortifications surrounding a castle.
EYECATCHER	see FOLLY
FOLLY	A useless and generally foolish building, erected in the grounds of wealthy eccentrics, especially in the 18c and 19c.
FOREBUILDING	Building against the keep containing a stairway to the entrance.
FORFEIT	see CONFISCATE
FORTALICE	Defined as 'a small outwork of a fortification'.
FOSSE	Ditch
GA	Printed guide available.
GARDEROBE	Toilet/latrine/privy.
GOTHIC	Architectural period commenced c.1755.
GR	Grid Reference.

HALL	Main domestic building.
HERRING-BONE	Masonry laid diagonally in zig-zag courses. (Herring-bone masonry was used by the Romans, Anglo-Saxons, Normans and later medieval builders, but where mentioned in this book the term refers to Norman work, the period decided upon after other features/documentary evidence of the castles have been considered.) See JBAA.27(1964) pp.4-13.
IRON AGE	Period c.600 B.C. to the Roman occupation.
JACOBEAN	Architectural period 1603-25.
JAMB	The straight side of a doorway, window, etc.
KEEP	Main tower of a castle.
KNIGHTS FEE	An amount of cash/land in return for which a tenant gave his service to the feudal army for 40 days, or performed castle-guard, castle work or escort duty.
LATRINE	see GARDEROBE
LICENCE TO CRENELLATE	A permit, usually from the King, to fortify an existing house, etc., or to build/rebuild a castle anew.
MACHICOULIS	Projecting parapets supported on CORBELS with openings designed for the downward discharge of missiles.
MARK	Medieval currency.
MEDIEVAL	Period 4c to 16c, but for use in this book the period commences c.1050.
MESSUAGE	see CAPITAL MESSUAGE
MIDDLE AGES	see MEDIEVAL
MINORITY	Heir/heiress under age, and the estates cared for by the Crown or someone designated by the Crown.
MOTTE	Steep-sided mound forming the main feature of an 11c/12c castle.
MULLION	Vertical post or upright dividing a window into two or more lights.
MULTIVALLATE	Having three or more lines of defence.
MURAL CHAMBER/ STAIR	Room/stair in the thickness of the wall.
NT	National Trust.
NEWEL STAIR	Spiral stairs.
NORMAN	Architectural period c.1050-1200.
OS	Ordnance Survey.
OTV	Open to visitors.
PALISADE	Defence of strong timber stakes set in the ground.
PARAPET	Low wall on outer side of a wider one.

PEEL/PELE	A small barn-like house, roughly built with thick DRYSTONE walls, also called bastle, stronghouse, stonehouse, or pelehouse. The term is often used inaccurately to describe the northern TOWERHOUSE.
PERPENDICULAR	Architectural period c.1377-1485.
PILASTER	Shallow solid support partly built into a wall as a buttress.
PIPE ROLL	Exchequer accounts, so called because they were rolled into a long pipe-like bundle.
PLINTH	Projecting base of a wall or column.
PN	Place name.
PORTCULLIS	An iron-shod wooden grille, suspended by chains which allows it to rise and fall in vertical grooves to block a passage or doorway.
POSTERN	Subsidiary gateway often concealed in case of surprise attacks by an enemy.
PROMONTORY FORT	A fort, usually IRON AGE, on a coastal promontory or the spur of a hill, and defended on one side by ramparts.
PUTLOG HOLES	Holes which supported timber scaffolding.
QUOIN	Dressed stones at the angles of buildings.
RESTORATION	Restoration of the Monarchy, 1660.
REVETTED	Faced with masonry, acting as a retaining wall.
RHOMBIC	Diamond shaped.
RINGWORK	Usually a roughly circular earthwork of a bank and ditch.
RUBBLE	Undressed stone not laid in regular courses.
SALLYPORT	see POSTERN
SCARP	Artificial cutting away of ground to form a slope.
SCHEDULED	see AM
SEGMENTAL	An arch of which the contour is a segment of a circle, but less than a semicircle.
SHELL KEEP	Wall surrounding a small area, usually the top of a MOTTE.
SIEGE CASTLE/WORK	A fortification set up close to a fortified place in order to harass and eventually take it by force.
SOLAR	Upper drawing-room of a medieval house.
STRING COURSE	A projecting horizontal band set in the surface of a wall.
TEMP	In the time of.
TOWERHOUSE	A stone tower of three or four storeys usually with a BARMKIN.
TREFOIL	Three-lobed figure.
TUDOR	Architectural period c.1500-c.1600, thus including ELIZABETHAN architecture.

TUMULUS	see BARROW
TURRET/TURRIS	Small tower.
TYMPANUM	Space between the lintel of a doorway, and the arch above it.
UNDERCROFT	A range of vaulted storerooms, etc., beneath the principal rooms.
UNIVALLATE	Defended by a single bank and ditch.
VALLUM	Rampart
VAULT	An arched roof of stone.
WARD	see BAILEY
WALL-WALK	Passage along wall top.

Millom Castle, a 14th-century fortified manor house.

Castles of England

OTHER VOLUMES IN THIS SERIES BY THE SAME AUTHOR

Published by Carel Press, 18 Chertsey Bank, Carlisle CA1 2QF

Northumberland/Durham/Cleveland/Tyne & Wear
Devon/Cornwall
Somerset/Dorset/Wiltshire/Avon
Lancashire/Cheshire/Greater Manchester/Merseyside
Yorkshire/Humberside/Cleveland
Hereford and Worcester/Gloucester/Avon
Derbyshire/Nottinghamshire/Leicestershire
Staffordshire/Warwickshire/West Midlands
Northants/Oxfordshire/Bucks/Berkshire
Lincolnshire/Norfolk
Suffolk/Essex
Bedfordshire/Cambridgeshire/Hertfordshire
Hampshire/Isle of Wight
Greater London/Surrey
Sussex/Kent
A Concise Index of Medieval Castle Sites in England

Note: Some of these volumes may be produced singly.

Shropshire is published by Shropshire Libraries and available from:
> The Publications Officer
> Shropshire Libraries
> Column House
> 7 London Road
> SHREWSBURY
> Shropshire SY2 6NW

Inside back cover: Bewcastle: the ruinous entrance.